T0330074

Theories and Models in Economics

Theories and Models in Economics

An Empirical Approach to Methodology

Hans Lind

Professor of Real Estate Economics, formerly at the Department of Real Estate and Construction Management, KTH Royal Institute of Technology, Stockholm, Sweden

Edward **Elgar**
PUBLISHING

Cheltenham, UK • Northampton, MA, USA

Published by
Edward Elgar Publishing Limited
The Lypiatts
15 Lansdown Road
Cheltenham
Glos GL50 2JA
UK

Edward Elgar Publishing, Inc.
William Pratt House
9 Dewey Court
Northampton
Massachusetts 01060
USA

A catalogue record for this book
is available from the British Library

Library of Congress Control Number: 2024930587

This book is available electronically in the **Elgar**online
Economics subject collection
http://dx.doi.org/10.4337/9781035332953

ISBN 978 1 0353 3294 6 (cased)
ISBN 978 1 0353 3295 3 (eBook)
Printed and bound by CPI Group (UK) Ltd, Croydon, CR0 4YY

Contents

1. Introduction and background to the empirical approach to methodology

Hopefully it is understandable that a person who has been thinking and writing about an issue on and off for 50 years, now wants to describe some kind of standpoint or conclusion. I started to read economics at Stockholm University in the fall of 1972 when I was studying in my last year at the KTH-Royal Institute of Technology. In the middle of the 1970s, I also studied philosophy for three years, in parallel with my studies in economics. I continued with economics later in the 1970s. Mathematics had always been one of my top subjects and I found it easy to follow the courses and understand the theories and models that was presented in the more advanced courses.

However, I had problems with understanding why economists were doing what they were doing. There were, of course, a lot of interesting results in the analysis of the mathematical models, but the link between knowing what happens in the models and understanding how the real world works was far from clear. I had a meeting with one of the professors in the Economics Department in 1976 and said that I wanted to write about methodology. I added that I had read philosophy of science, so I thought I had the right background. I was stupid enough to add that methodology was discussed much more in other social science subjects, e.g. sociology. His comment was roughly that sociologists had to discuss methodology as it was a less developed social science, but that such methodological discussions weren't needed in economics. The established methods were that you build mathematical models if you were doing a "theoretical" study and carried out econometric analysis if you did empirical studies.

I had also tried to discuss the role of mathematical models with some colleagues at the Department of Economics and I especially remember two comments. One was: "What else should I do if I want to do a theoretical study?" As I had read the Kuhn theory of paradigms and scientific revolutions, the answer did not surprise me: if you are working in a certain paradigm, it is difficult to see that there can be other approaches. Another colleague, now world famous, said: "I do not want to think about this. The leading journals publish this kind of article, and the leading economists write such articles, and that is enough for me." I thought that this was a very rational answer: What are really the odds that a sceptical young economist is right and almost all leading economists are wrong? It cannot be totally wrong if "all" leading economists work in this way.

I wrote several papers on methodological issue in Swedish in the early 1980s, but as interest in this issue was low in the department, I started to work with Professor Peter Bohm on a project on experimental and quasi-experimental methods in economics. He was really ahead of his time, as can be seen in our 1993 paper entitled "Policy evaluation quality: A quasi-experimental study of regional employment subsidies in Sweden" (Bohm & Lind 1993). In parallel, I continued with my methodological studies but with a specific twist: I wanted to make empirical studies on how economists actually argued. Too much methodology in economics was written without any solid empirical base in studies about what mainstream economists actually do, how they actually argue and how they argue for doing what they do. I did not want to "flog a dead horse" which is what I thought many heterodox economists were doing. One thing I learned from my philosophical studies was to read and carefully examine the arguments put forward. This was useful when looking at economic articles and trying to understand why the researcher had used certain methods and made certain claims.

In the late 1980s, I carried out several empirical studies about mainstream economics that were later were included in a monograph written in Swedish, with the English title "The research strategy in modern economics". This was approved for a PhD in 1990. Some years later, I also made a similar type of study of institutional economists, which led to the article "The myth of institutionalist method" (Lind 1993a).

I had a short moment of fame in the methodology of economics circles around 1990. I had written an English version of one of chapters in the Swedish monograph. The paper had the title "A case study of normal research in theoretical economics" (later published in *Economics and Philosophy*, Lind 1992) and it was read by McCloskey (Donald at that time, now Deirdree) and she thought my paper was fantastic and the best she had read in this area in a long time. In several of her articles and books in the early 1990s you can find reference to my unpublished work, for example in McCloskey (1994). She made a nice a summary of the result of my study by saying that the typical theoretical article in economics is "Rigorous in the middle, but touchie-feely on the ends". There is a rigorous mathematical part in the middle of the article, but both the introductory section motivating the model and the final section where conclusions are drawn are rather vague. I asked McCloskey to write down her comments and that enthusiastic letter was very important for convincing the Department of Economics at Stockholm University that my work on methodology should be enough for a doctoral degree.

One illustration of the usefulness of looking closer at how economists actually argue is the following. In many textbooks and in many discussions at the time, economists made reference to Milton Friedman's methodological views, which were interpreted as saying that a theory should be evaluated by the predictions of the model and not by the realism of the assumptions. But when I looked closer at the selected theoretical articles, I found that the most common argument put forward for why this new article was an improvement compared with earlier articles was that the new model was more realistic on some important dimension. And no one argued that their theoretical model was better than earlier models because it gave better predictions.

Continuing with methodology as a primary research area did not seem very attractive to me. No Economics department in Sweden was interested in this area, and I were not interested in moving abroad. I had started reading Economics because I wanted to understand how economies function and I was primarily interested in more applied work. This made me return to KTH in 1992 and eventually I became professor of Real Estate Economics.

The interest in methodology was still with me and, some years later, it struck me that if you want to evaluate what we learn from "theoretical" mathematical models in Economics it has to be models in an area where you are an expert. If you are not an expert in the field, you cannot know if the analysis of the mathematical model increased our knowledge and helped us understand how a specific market works, or helped us understand the effects of a specific policy. As I had several publications in housing journals about rent regulation (rent control), both conceptual and empirical (Lind 2001, 2003), I thought that looking at economics articles with mathematical models of rent regulation could be interesting. This idea eventually led to the article "The story and the model done: An evaluation of mathematical models of rent control" (Lind 2007). As can be seen in the reference list I also had a few other publications in the methodology field.

When I retired from KTH some years ago, I returned to the area of "empirical methodological studies" and results from these studies form the main empirical base of this book. I started by studying Nobel Prize in Economics.[1] The hypothesis was that understanding what was seen as important contributions could help us understand the field in question, but it was also a more general curiosity about what one could learn from these texts. Then it struck me that comparing the motivations for awarding the Nobel Prize motivations in Economics with the motivations in Physics could lead to interesting results about similarities and differences between Economics (a Social Science) and

---

[1]   I call it the Nobel Prize in Economics even though this is not formally correct. It was not part of the prizes in Alfred Nobel's will but was created in 1968 by the Swedish Riksbank and the correct name is "the Prize in Economic Sciences in Memory of Alfred Nobel".

Physics (a Natural Science), so I carefully read the motivations for the Physics prize for the years that the Economics prize has existed. The results from the analysis of the motivations for awarding the Nobel Prize are the core of the empirical base in, especially, Chapters 2, 3, 5 and 8 of this book. As described in the Appendix several types of material are published about the Nobel Prize winners. In the comparisons between Economics and Physics, I have only used what in the Appendix is called the short motivations and the official motivation. In the chapters where I only focus on Economics, I have also used the speech to the laureate when the prize is handed out, articles about the laureate in the *Scandinavian Journal of Economics* and the Advanced information that has been published since 1995.

The studies of the Nobel Prize motivations give information about the exceptional economists and their contributions. But if you want to understand a science you should, of course, also look closer at more ordinary scientific works. I therefore selected 100 full-length articles published in *American Economic Review* in 1990 and 100 articles published in 2020. I started with issue 1, 1990, and issue 1, 2020, and downloaded all articles until I had 100 articles. I had to add a few articles from 1991 to reach 100. The material was then analysed from a number of different perspectives. The results from this study are presented in several of the following chapters, especially in Chapters 4, 6 and 7. In the Appendix more details are given about both the study of Nobel Prize motivations and the study of the articles in the *American Economic Review*.

This book is written with two specific audiences in mind. The book should be of interest to those both inside and outside Economics who wants to understand how economists work and especially learn about the use of theories and models in Economics. As I see it, there are both criticisms and defences of Economics that are not based on systematic knowledge of what economists really do and really claim in their research.

The book should also be suitable for courses in the methodology of economics as a more empirical complement to the existing methodology books that typically start from various philosophical theories and positions and try to relate what economists do and claim to these theories. There are, for example, a number of classical methodology books that look at economics from the perspective of positivism, Kuhn's theory of paradigms, Popperian falsificationism or the Lakatos theory of research programmes.

The structure of the book is as follows. In order to understand what economists do, it is important to think about the characteristics of the object that economics studies. In Chapter 2, I formulate the hypothesis that this object has a chaos-like structure. This hypothesis is tested by deriving a number of implications about what we should find if we compare motivations for Nobel

Prizes in Economics and Physics. The tests showed that there were statistically significant differences supporting the hypothesis about a chaos-like object.

The subsequent two chapters describe what economists do in their research. Chapter 3 is based on the study of Nobel Prize motivations and categorizes path-breaking contributions – contributions that motivate a Nobel Prize. Six different types of contributions were found.

Chapter 4 focuses on what Kuhn calls normal science and categorizes articles published in *American Economic Review*, 1990 and 2020. Three types of articles were found: those where the core was an analysis of relations in a mathematical model, those that presented an empirical study without any explicit "theoretical" model, and a third group that included both such a model and an empirical study. Over time the first group has shrunk while the second group has increased and also included more experimental and quasi-experimental studies.

In Chapter 5, I compare two views of how science develops over time. Kuhn's model of scientific revolutions and Laudan's more incremental model where important elements can be replaced, but where the rest of a research tradition is kept intact. The data from the Nobel Prize motivations strongly support Laudan's view. Mathematical methods were, for example, introduced without changing behavioural assumptions, and new behavioural assumptions were later introduced but without changing the methods used.

Chapter 6 focuses on theory in economics. After looking at how theory is defined in some advanced dictionaries, I investigate how theory is used in AER-articles. It is, for example, found that the word *theory/theoretical* is used rather sparsely. One issue studied is the relation between theory (theoretical models) and empirical studies, and it is found that this relation is rather weak. There is also a section about the meaning and use of theoretical frameworks.

Chapter 7 is about models, and while the word *theory/theoretical* is used rather sparsely, the word *model/modelling* is used about ten times more often. Here, I also start with the meaning of models according to some advanced dictionaries and with an investigation of how the words are used in the AER-articles. Two main interpretations are mathematical models that are studied in "theoretical" articles, and empirical models that are the base for statistical estimation. The focus in the rest of the chapter is on the first type of model analysis and some views from the methodological literature are presented. I argue that a Bayesian framework can be used to evaluate the empirical value of the mathematical models: the result in the mathematical model can be seen as "new information" and the questions is then how much it is rational to change the probability of specific empirical assertions. Realism in assumptions, robustness of the results and lack of competing hypotheses are then important aspects, besides the result being supported by "common sense".

In Chapter 8, a case study of Krugman's New trade theory illustrates how a new idea can be established through a combination of simple general equilibrium models, empirical studies and common sense.

Chapter 9 summarizes the main points of the earlier chapter and presents some concluding reflections. If the final aim of science is to evaluate how probable various empirical statements are, then a Bayesian framework seems interesting. All kinds of studies produce new information, and the question is how much it is rational to change the probability of specific empirical statements given this new information. The new information can be anything from a result that a certain relation holds in a mathematical model to statements in an interview with someone working in the field. My final hypothesis is that there is diminishing marginal utility of each specific kind of information in relation to a specific empirical issue. If a lot of mathematical models have been built, then maybe interviews or case studies can change the probabilities of empirical statements more. And the other way around, if a lot of information from interviews and case-studies is available, then analysing sufficient conditions for a certain relation in a mathematical model could increase our knowledge more. An implication of this is that it is not rational to have a general opinion about what is the best method in economics or about "the role of mathematical models" in economics.

2. What characterizes the object that Economics studies?

2.1 INTRODUCTION

In order to understand what economists do and why they do it, it is important to form an opinion about the object that Economics studies. Is this object different from what, for example, the natural sciences study? And how should such a question be answered? The idea behind this chapter is that if there are differences between the object that Economics studies compared with what a natural science, such as Physics, studies, then this should show up in motives for awarding the Nobel Prize. What kind of contributions are made and what are seen as important contributions? Have the researchers' made the same kind of contribution in the different fields?

The strategy in this chapter is therefore to first formulate a hypothesis about what characterizes the object that Economics studies (compared with, at least, large parts of Physics). A number of testable implications are then derived concerning what we should expect to find in the motivations for awarding the Nobel Prize if this hypothesis is correct. Finally, these implications are tested to see if there are statistically significant differences between the motivations as suggested by the hypothesis. The Nobel Prizes from 1969–2018 have been used in this study. Only Physics prizes for the period when the prize in Economics has been in existence have been included.

It is well known that if one does a large number of statistical tests then one will, by chance, find some statistically significant relations. Let me therefore say that there are no unreported non-significant tests. Only the hypotheses formulated in advance have been investigated. I have also split the material into two halves and tested the hypotheses for the first and last 25 years separately. As the same patterns were found in both periods I will not comment on these results.

2.2   THE HYPOTHESIS: AN OBJECT WITH A CHAOS-LIKE STRUCTURE

The central hypothesis is that Economics studies an object that has a "chaos-like structure", while large parts of Physics does not. In order to make this claim more precise it is necessary to look closer at two concepts: complexity and chaos.

A typical definition of complexity is the following from Herbert Simon (quoted from Kirman 2016, p. 545):

> Roughly by a complex system I mean one made up of a large number of parts that interact in a non-simple way.

Rickles, Hawe and Shiell (2007) presents a somewhat more explicit definition:

> Complex systems are highly composite ones, built up from very large numbers of mutually interacting subunits (that are often composites themselves) whose repeated interactions result in rich collective behaviour that feeds back into the behaviour of the individual parts. (p. 933)

A similar definition can be found in Colander and Kupers (2014, p. 67). There is, of course, a certain amount of vagueness in these definitions: what are, for example, "very large numbers"? From the perspective of my study, this vagueness should not matter.

Complexity does not, however, exclude predictability. In a stable complex system, especially one that can be experimented on, it might be possible to find the laws that govern the system and predict how it will behave, even though there are many interacting components.

Turning to the concept of chaos, the *Stanford Encyclopaedia of Philosophy*[1] starts by noting:

> The big news about chaos is supposed to be that the smallest of changes in a system can result in very large differences in that system's behaviour.

This is clarified in terms of something called SDIC: Sensitive Dependence on Initial Conditions.

My hypothesis is then that the object that Economics studies is "chaos-like", which can be described in the following way. The economy is a complex system with many interacting parts and where relatively small differences in

---

[1]   https://plato.stanford.edu/entries/chaos/, entry from 2015 (accessed 10 October 2019).

the characteristics of the system will affect how it will react to various changes. It should also be added that the economy is a system that changes over time. Colander and Kupers (2014, p. 4) write:

> those very choices will themselves influence the dynamics of the system, as well as people's tastes and preferences. It won't be the same system once the policies are under way, and that very fact can bring about both opportunities and unforeseen consequences.

The same idea is described in the following way on the website of the Complexity Economics Programme at INET, University of Oxford:[2]

> a distributed network of dynamically interacting, heterogeneous agents, whose behaviours, strategies and relationships evolve over time.

Even if there are underlying deterministic relations, it would be impossible to identify these if it is a complex system, where small differences can have a large effect, and where the relations change over time. There is simply no way of finding out what these underlying deterministic relations are, as it will not be possible to collect enough data until the system has changed. This is especially true if experimental studies are difficult to carry out in many parts of the system. From the standpoint of empirical science, the consequence of these characteristics of the object is that there are no stable empirical laws between observable characteristics and only very limited predictability.

For example, a certain economic policy might have one consequence during one period of time, but another in a later period. A standard example is Keynesian economic policy that is often described as working well during its first 25 years, but did not work after that. When actors' learn about a policy and change their expectations and behaviour, the policy will not work in the same way anymore. A policy that works well in one country, might not work in another, even though the countries look similar, because there are "minor" remaining differences that affect the consequences. There might be institutional differences or differences in what people expect of the policy and therefore in how they react. Another classical example is that how people will react to a tax-change will depend on whether they believe that the change will be temporary or permanent – and what they think the effect of the tax change will be on their future income.

The simplest explanation for the chaos-like structure of an economy is that behaviour depends on expectations, and these are neither easy to observe nor

---

[2]   https://www.inet.ox.ac.uk/research/programmes/complexity-economics (accessed 10 October 2019).

necessarily stable over even a short period of time. A further example is that the consequence of reducing the price of a product will depend on whether consumers think that there will soon be further price reductions or not. People might also need to form expectations about other peoples' expectations, and this can contribute to making relations between observable economic factors unstable. Various game-theoretic situations contribute to this uncertainty about relations between observable factors, such as prices and production, as the rational strategy of one firm depends on what it thinks other companies will do. In a longer perspective, changes in the institutional or industrial structure, or changes in other countries can affect the effect of a policy or the effect of an event in a specific country. Suddenly, for example, trade with a certain country might be forbidden.

It should be underlined that this dividing line between Economics and (large parts of) Physics is not necessarily a line between social science and natural science. Chaos-like structures seem to occur in natural sciences, and it is easy to find claims such as

> Meteorology, and the prediction of weather and climate, is a classic example of such an unpredictable (chaotic) system.[3]

The chaos-like structure does not preclude rather stable relations during relatively long periods of time, but there will never be any precise stable relations, and rather quickly exceptions to a specific relation will be found. It should be emphasized that the same holds for probabilistic relations; for example, that a certain consequence occurs with probability P. The chaos-like structure means that this probability will not be stable over time and will not be the same in different countries.

Rodrik (2015, p. 67) writes "In economics, context is all", and he also writes the following, even though he does not discuss more in detail why this is the case: "Beyond trite generalities such as 'incentives matter' or 'beware of unintended consequences', there are few immutable truths in economics" (Rodrik 2015, p. 148) and that ".. no social science should claim to make predictions and be judged on that basis" (p. 184). All of these statements are logical if Economics studies a chaos-like object.

---

[3]   See, for example, https://www.encyclopedia.com/environment/energy-government-and-defense-magazines/chaos-theory-and-meteorological-predictions

2.3   IMPLICATIONS CONCERNING THE USE OF CERTAIN WORDS

2.3.1   Framework

In both sciences we should expect to find hypotheses about causal factors and about relations. In Physics there can, following the arguments above, be theories stating that there are certain exact laws of nature, certain exact mathematical relations or certain definitive structures or processes.

In a science that studies a chaos-theoretic object, a theory cannot be something that contains such definitive claims, as there always will be exceptions, or at least some situations where factor A is the most important and other situations where factor B is the most important. *A theory can then be expected to be more like a framework*, that in a systematic way describes factors that probably are important in most cases. Rodrik (2015, p. 4) writes about "applying simple economic frameworks" and that "general theories ... are a way of organizing our thought". A theory in a science that studies a chaos-like object helps the scientist to make a structured investigation of specific cases or specific periods. It tells the researchers what one should check if one wants to avoid mistakes.

The implication of this is that formulations where theories are described as frameworks, and that the contribution of the laureate is to have developed such a framework for explanation and understanding, will be more common in Economics motivations than in Physics motivations.

In the tables below, the first number is the number of years (of the 50 years studied) where the word occurs in the relevant texts. The number in parentheses is the total number of occurrences.

The tables below only includes cases where a framework is used in a context where theory or the contribution of the laureate are discussed. In the Economics texts there were, for example, references to the legal or institutional frameworks and such cases are not included. In Table 2.1 it is clear that the implication holds, and a statistical t-test showed that difference is statistically significant at the 5 per cent level.[4] In Chapter 6, on theory, I will return more in detail to questions about what a framework is and how it can be used.

---

[4]   In the rest of this chapter all differences presented are statistically significant at the 5 per cent level. As mentioned in the introduction, more details about how the study was carried out can be found in the appendix.

Table 2.1   *The use of the word framework: number of years and number of occurrences*

	Economics	Physics
Framework	22 (29)	6 (7)

2.3.2   Describe/Description

If a science studies an object that is not chaos-like, there are facts and stable relations between variables, and it should therefore be more natural to say that a theory *describes* an object or a law. For a chaos-like object, there will always be exceptions and it is then not so natural to say that the theory describes something. The hypothesis is then that the word *description* will be more common in the Physics motivations. As mentioned above, I have checked all occurrences and only included occurrences in contexts where theories and contributions of the laurate are discussed. Table 2.2 shows that the material supports the hypothesis: the word *describe/description* is actually used much more often in the Physics motivations.

Table 2.2   *The use of the word describe/description: number of years and number of occurrences*

	Economics	Physics
Description	18 (45)	33 (113)

2.3.3   Confirm/confirmation

If a science studies an object that is chaos-like, theories might get support and be correct in many situations, but it will seldom be the case that such a theory can be said to be *confirmed*. It should be more natural to say that theories about, for example, the structure of atoms or about the occurrence of certain phenomena in space are confirmed by certain observations. The implication of this argument is therefore that the word confirm should be found more often in Physics than in the Economics. Table 2.3 shows that this implication also holds.

Table 2.3   *The use of the word confirm/confirmation: number of years and number of occurrences*

	Economics	Physics
Confirmation	9 (12)	21 (39)

The real difference between Economics and Physics may actually be larger than this table shows, as it is possible to question some of the Economics cases that have been included. In some included cases, what was said to be confirmed were rather general statements and not any precise hypothesis. An example from the 2002 Economics prize is the following: "Subsequent research contains numerous applications which extend this theory and confirm the importance of signalling on different markets". In another of the included Economics cases (the 1983 prize to Arrow) the statement that is said to be confirmed is not an empirical statement: "In this model, Arrow and Debreu managed to prove the existence of equilibrium prices, i.e., they confirmed the internal logical consistency of Smith's and Walras's model of the market economy".

2.3.4   Analyse/Analysis

It is not so easy to describe what scientists that study a chaos-like object really do. They cannot formulate laws or formulate theories that describe something in precise terms, as there are no stable relations. But what they do is to present analytical frameworks, point out (neglected) things that often are an explanation for something and that are important for understanding a certain phenomenon (see Chapter 6). A rather vague word such as "analysis" – or having "analysed" something – should be a more suitable description of what a scientist does when they study a chaos-like object. The word *analyse* or *analysis* should therefore be more common in the Economics motivations than in the Physics motivations.

Here, I have both looked at the short motivations – typically one of two sentences – and the longer texts where the reason for awarding the price is described. The results are presented in Tables 2.4 and 2.5, and also in this case the implications from the hypothesis hold.

If we look at the short motivations for awarding the prize there really is a dramatic difference: the word *analyse/analysis* is used in more than half of the motivations in Economics, but in none of the Physics motivations. The total number of occurrences in the longer texts are 16 times higher than in the Physics motivations.

Table 2.4   *The use of the word analyse/analysis in the short motivations:*
                   number of years

	Economics	Physics
Analysis (in short motivation)	27	0

Table 2.5   *The use of the word analyse/analysis in the longer*
                   motivations: number of years and number of occurrences

	Economics	Physics
Analysis	50 (605)	18 (37)

2.4   WHAT KIND OF REGULARITY HAS THE LAUREATE FOUND?

In the section above, the implications of the hypothesis concerned the use
of specific words and the differences between the Economics and Physics
motivations could then be tested statistically. In this section, we come to implications that are more difficult to test, as simple word counts are not enough.
How the analyses have been done is described more in detail in the appendix.

Both Economics and Physics look for regularities. If a science studies
a chaos-like object, there are, however, no stable precise empirical regularities.
This implies that the Nobel Prize winners in economics cannot have been
awarded the prize for having found such stable precise empirical regularities.
Such cases should, however ,be rather common among the winners of the
Physics prize.

In Economics, one should instead expect that prizes have been awarded for
having found more qualitative relations, such as that the (neglected) factor
X is important for understanding a certain phenomenon Y, but that the exact
strength of the relation might differ between countries and periods. The claims
in economics are more like a recommendation for researchers: "If you want
to understand the development of phenomena Y in a certain region during
a certain period, then do not forget to check the development of factor X."

I have gone through the texts looking for statements about regularities
that the laurates have found and collected all statements of this type and then
looked closer at these to see if they are in line with the implications described
above.

The result was very much in line with the implications of the hypothesis
about a chaos-like structure. No one has received the Nobel Prize in Economics
for finding a quantitative empirical law. There was only one comment about

"the nature of economic relations" and that was found in the speech to Milton Friedman. The statement in the quotation below is consistent with the hypothesis about a chaos-like object:

> Unfortunately the social sciences – despite high ambitions – can never reach the hoped for exactitude. The enormous capabilities of people and governments to create new complications, new contradictions and conflicts, are inexhaustible and go far above and beyond the economists' powers to bring order into the system.

In Table 2.6, there are examples of the more qualitative regularities that the Nobel Prize winners in Economics have found.

Table 2.6   Examples of statements about empirical relations in Economics prize motivations

Year/person	Empirical relation
1974 Hayek	Market economy and possibility of rational calculation
1976 Friedman	Money supply and inflation, permanent income and consumption
1977 Ohlin	Factor proportions and trade
1982 Stigler	Group interests and regulation
1987 Solow	A number of determinants of growth
1991 Coase	Transaction cost and contract form
1993 North	Institutional structure and economic growth
1995 Lucas	Inflationary expectations and inflation
1998 Sen	Real income losses and famines
1999 Mundell	Exchange rate system and effects of macroeconomic policy
2001 Spence	Asymmetric information and signalling behaviour
2002 Kahneman	Loss aversion and behaviour under uncertainty
2008 Krugman	Taste for diversity, economies of scale and intra-industry trade
2009 Williamson	Asset specificity and vertical integration
2013 Fama	New information and change in asset value
2016 Hart & Holmstrom	Measurability and the use of incentive contracts

In the Physics motivations, a number of statements about specific quantitative relations between variables were found, just as we should expect if the object under study does not have a chaos-like structure. Table 2.7 gives some examples, and they have been selected in order to show that such statements can be found during the whole period under study.

Table 2.7   Examples of statements about empirical relations in Physics

Year	Empirical relation
1969	Some law must exist which prevents the strong forces acting when they disintegrate into other particles. Gell-Mann discovered this law ... Elementary particles can be transformed in others by the strong and the electromagnetic interactions only if the total hypercharge is conserved.
1974	Ryle's measurements enable us to conclude that a steady-state model of the Universe cannot be accepted. The Cosmos on a large scale has to be described by dynamic, evolutionary models.
1977	This theory is not universally valid, however, and a famous exception is provided by nickel oxide, which according to band theory ought to be a metallic conductor but in reality is an insulator. Mott has shown how this can be explained by means of a refined theory which takes the electron–electron interaction into account.
1982	Wilson's theory for critical phenomena gave a complete theoretical description of the behaviour close to the critical point and also gave methods to calculate numerically the crucial quantities
1985	He discovered from his experimental data that a relation that had been assumed to hold only approximately seemed to hold with an exceptionally high accuracy and in this way the discovery of the quantized Hall effect was made.
1988	Demonstration of the doublet structure of the leptons through the discovery of the muon neutrino. Thus, a new law of Nature had been discovered.
1993	This is because the orbiting period of the pulsar around its companion gradually diminishes with time – extremely little, but in exactly the way the general theory of relativity predicts,
1999	They have, in particular, shown how the theory may be used for precise calculations of physical quantities.
2003	Superfluid 3He can exist in three phases called A, A1, and B. The type of phase is determined by pressure, temperature and magnetic field according to the figure's phase diagram
2006	Extremely small differences of this kind in the temperature of the cosmic background radiation – in the range of a hundred-thousandth of a degree – offer an important clue to how the galaxies came into being.
2013	They had indeed found the particle. The Standard Model was complete and it had been found that Nature follows precisely that law that Brout, Englert and Higgs had created.
2017	The wave's form was exactly as predicted.

The examples from Physics are of several somewhat different types: that they are precise relations, that there are exactly measured constants, that a certain precisely described feature is exactly as a theory predict and that this makes it possible to predict certain things with very high precision.

2.5   THE USE OF MATHEMATICS

There is a lot of mathematics in both Physics and Economics. The hypothesis here is that they are using mathematics in different ways because they (mostly) study objects with different structures.

If a scientist studies an object that is not chaos-like – where precise and stable empirical regularities exist – then mathematics can be used to describe these relations. The scientist presents a hypothesis in mathematical form, and it is then claimed that this mathematical structure describes the actual relations. More advanced mathematical methods are introduced if, by using them, it is possible to formulate exact theories that fit the data better. Formulations referring to exact mathematical descriptions of what is believed to be an actual relation should therefore be found in the physics motivations, but such formulations should not be found in the economics motivations.

But how can a scientist use mathematics if they study a chaos-like object? The first use is, of course, in econometric analysis. Somewhat simplified, one can say that the researchers propose an equation that includes the factors the researchers think are the most important ones. The researchers then estimate the parameters of the model, and that shows how strong these relations are in a specific context. The result is an estimated quantitative relation, but it is not expected that the quantitative parameters will be exactly the same if the relation is estimated for another time and place – or even if it is estimated with another data-material for the same time and place. As discussed above, even if it is a chaos-like object, quantitative relations might hold, at least approximately, for a certain period of time in a specific place, and might be used as a help when predictions have to be made.

This first type of use of mathematics in Economics is related to the use of statistics. An implication is then that statistics should be mentioned much more often in the motivations for Nobel Prizes in economics than in the Physics motivations. When there are determinate relations it is more a matter of measuring than of estimating statistically how strong a certain relation is and investigating if parameters are statistically significant. I therefore checked how often the word *statistics* or *statistical* was used in the respective motivations. The result, presented in Table 2.8, is consistent with the hypothesized difference.

Table 2.8   The use of the word statistics/statistical

	Economics	Physics
Statistics	28 (138)	5 (8)

Mathematics can also be used for building quantitative simulation models, where the model-builder is satisfied if the assumptions are such that the result of the simulation is judged to be interesting and relevant. But this use has not been important in the motivations for awarding the Nobel Prize, even if some prizes were awarded for developing statistical methods – see the next chapter.

There is, however, a third use of mathematics in economics and this is when mathematics is used for "theoretical purposes". Instead of using mathematics to make claims about empirical relations, mathematics is used for finding (interesting) logically sufficient conditions for a certain relation to hold. The economist builds a mathematical model and proves, using mathematical methods, that certain relations hold in the model. The following example can illustrate a shift from claims about empirical laws to claims about sufficient conditions for a certain relation to be provable (that the relation is logically necessary given the assumptions).

Let us start with the classical "law of demand", saying that when the price is reduced the quantity sold will increase. A first counterexample is that if incomes fall even more, then the quantity sold might fall. In order to remove the problem of interaction with other changes, a ceteris paribus clause is added: the law only holds if everything else that might influence consumption is constant. The good may however be what Veblen called a Snob good, and the status value of the good can then fall when the price falls, leading to a fall in the consumed quantity when the price is reduced. The good might also be a Giffen good, where the income effect dominates over the substitution effect: the classical example was that increasing potato prices led to higher consumption of potatoes in Ireland during the famine, as a poor household now could only afford potatoes. Furthermore, if customers believe there is a relation between price and quality, or that the customers believe that the reduction in price will be followed by even more price reductions (for a durable good), it might be the case that a price reduction leads to a fall in sales.

The "law of demand" would then be formulated something like the following: "If the price is reduced, the quantity sold will increase, ceteris paribus, if it is not a Snob good or a Giffen good, and if customers do not judge quality from price and do not expect a further fall in prices". But there might of course be other factors that can counteract the classical law of demand: one cannot be sure that even this rather complex empirical relation really is a true law.

In this situation, it is tempting for a scientist looking for certainty to reformulate the question. Instead of looking for a more and more complex credible empirical hypothesis, the economist looks for a set of conditions that are sufficient for proving that in this case – a reduction in price leads to an increase in sales. This change could be called the Samuelsonian turn in economics, and after that turn the role of the theoretical economist becomes to investigate logical sufficient conditions for a relation to hold – or for it not to hold. The theoretical economist shows that given the set of assumptions A, a relation between B and C holds (or an equilibrium exist, etc.).

A mathematical model where it is proven that, given certain assumptions, a specific relation holds can however be used in two very different ways.[5]

1. In the first case, the central assumptions are a bold empirical claim, such as the idea that the universe started with a Big Bang. From this hypothesis, together with other assumptions believed to be at least approximately true, observable relations are derived. These are then investigated and, if they are found to be true, this supports the assumptions made. This is the standard hypothetical-deductive method that is expected to be found in Physics.

2. In the second case, the ambition is to build a mathematical model that describes a "credible world" (to use the term from Sugden 2000) and then relations in this model are derived. In this use of a mathematical model, the fact that the relation holds in a credible world is an argument for believing that the relation holds in reality. The credible model might include assumptions that are known to be false, but that does not matter as long as these assumptions are believed to be harmless. The primary purpose of the model building is not, as in case (1) above, to argue that certain assumptions are true. The model is instead primarily used to argue that *the proven relations are empirically credible*, as the relation is proven to hold in a credible model. Rodrik (2015, p. 12) writes "A modeler builds an artificial world" and then Rodrik describes in detail the uses of mathematical models in modern economics (see Rodrik 2015, Chapter 2-4). This kind of model and the claims made by the researcher building the model will be discussed more in detail in Chapter 7.

Summing up, one implications of the arguments about mathematics presented above is that in the Physics motivations it will more often be said that *mathematics is used to describe what is believed to be quantitative empirical relations*. In the Economics motivations, we should expect to find more references to *economists having proved that something holds in a model, and that they have presented sufficient conditions for something to hold*. More advanced mathematics is useful in Economics because then you can prove things in more complex models, while in Physics more advanced mathematics is important when the object under study behaves in a way that makes advanced mathematics necessary for describing how the world works.

The arguments presented above imply that in Economics mathematics primarily will be mentioned in relation to formulations where a relation is proven in a mathematical model. In Physics it will be most common with formulations

---

[5]   See Lind (1992) for an earlier version of this argument in a comparison between idealizations in Economics and Physics.

where mathematics is used for describing empirical relations. Table 2.9 shows the result of classifying all places where mathematics is mentioned into each of these two categories and also a third category ("other") where references to mathematics are more general.

Table 2.9   Different contexts in which mathematics are mentioned

	Number of years mentioned: Economics	Number of years mentioned: Physics
Proofs in models	17	0
Empirical relations	1	11
Others	6	7

The Economics case that is classified as describing an empirical relation is not very specific. It comes from the 2011 prize to Sargent where it was said (emphasis added): "Sargent has examined these issues using a three-step method. His first step involves developing a structural macroeconomic model, i.e., an *accurate mathematical description of the economy*." No specific example is, however, given of an accurate mathematical description.

In order to make it easier for the reader to understand what lies behind the classification in Table 2.9, a number of examples of the first type of claim in the Economics motivations can be found in Table 2.10. Examples of the other type of claim from the Physics motivations can be found in Table 2.11.

Table 2.10   Examples of statements classified as referring to proofs in
mathematical models: Economics

Year	
1972	For example, he and Debreu were the first to be able to demonstrate, in a mathematically stringent manner, the conditions which must be fulfilled if a neoclassical general equilibrium system is to have a unique and economically meaningful solution.
1985	A stringent, mathematical formulation of this hypothesis led to a number of conclusions that could not be drawn from earlier theories, for example, that a person's saving is not determined only by their income, but also by their wealth, their expected future income, and their age.
1987	The article contains a mathematical model (in the form of a differential equation) describing how increased capital stock generates greater per capita production ... This means that, in the long term, the economy will approach a condition of identical growth rates for capital, labour and total production (on condition that there is no technological progress).
1988	By formulating rigorous mathematical models, it is possible to investigate the conditions under which social efficiency, equilibrium and stability can be attained in an economy with decentralized decisions made by independent consumers and producers

Year	
1994	Game theory is a mathematical method for analysing strategic interaction
2005	Robert Aumann's primary contributions consist of using the tools of mathematical analysis to develop concepts and hypotheses, provide them with concise formulations and draw precise conclusions.
2010	In the 1960s, researchers had already begun to use mathematical models to study the best possible way in which a buyer can try to find an acceptable price. In a renowned article from 1971, Peter Diamond examined how prices are formed on a market where buyers look for the best possible price and sellers simultaneously set their best price while taking buyers' search behaviour into account.
2012	The notion of stability is a central concept in cooperative game theory, an abstract area of mathematical economics which seeks to determine how any constellation of rational individuals might cooperatively choose an allocation... Gale and Shapley proved mathematically that this algorithm always leads to a stable matching.

Table 2.11   Examples of statements classified as referring to description of empirical regularities: Physics

Year	
1973	Electrons are described mathematically by the solutions of a wave equation, the Schrödinger equation.
1980	Symmetries are science's lodestars and symmetry principles act as guiding rules to help us discover the mathematical laws of Nature.
1991	De Gennes has shown that mathematical models, developed for studying simpler systems, are applicable also to such complicated systems. De Gennes has discovered relations between different, seemingly quite unrelated, fields of physics – connections which nobody has seen before. These variations follow a strict mathematical rule, which near the so-called critical temperature, where the magnet ceases to be magnetic, attains a very special form.
1999	The two researchers are being awarded the Nobel Prize for having placed particle physics theory on a firmer mathematical foundation. They have in particular shown how the theory may be used for precise calculations of physical quantities.
2003	...was able to show mathematically how the order parameter can describe vortices and how the external magnetic field can penetrate the material along the channels in these vortices. Guided by a deep physical intuition they went on to formulate mathematical equations whose solution determines the order in a superconductor. They found good agreement with what had been measured for superconductors known at the time.
2006	The same type of quantum mechanical fluctuations result in the constant creation and annihilation of particles of matter and antimatter in what we normally think of as empty space. This however is one of those aspects of physics that cannot readily be understood without using mathematics.

Year	
2008	Spontaneous symmetry violation that described superconductivity was later translated by Nambu into the world of elementary particles, and his mathematical tools now permeate all theories concerning the Standard Model.
2016	They have used advanced mathematical methods to study unusual phases, or states, of matter, such as superconductors, superfluids or thin magnetic films. The laws of physics are universal, and they are formulated in the language of mathematics
	A mathematically formulated theory is quantitative and can therefore often be used to, in detail and with high precision, explain and predict the results of experiments. But in the natural sciences, beauty is not enough – mathematics is full of beautiful results. Truth is also necessary.

Note especially the last quotation from the Physics motivation in 2016 "A mathematically formulated theory is quantitative and can therefore often be used to, in detail and with high precision, explain and predict the results of experiments."

Summing up, there is a clear pattern in the formulations about mathematics in the Economics and Physics motivations: in ("theoretical") economics mathematics is primarily used for proving relations in models and in physics mathematics is used to formulate (hypotheses about) empirical relations. The observed pattern is what should be expected if one science studies a chaos-like object while the other does not.

Even though it had nothing to do with testing any hypothesis, I checked – just out of curiosity – how often mathematics as such was mentioned in the Nobel Prize motivations. The result can be found in Table 2.12.

Table 2.12   Occurrences of the word mathematics/mathematical

	Number of years	Number of occurrences
Economics	20	64
Physics	14	47

It can be seen that mathematics is mentioned more often in the Economics motivations. When investigating whether there was a difference between the first and the last 25 years, it was found that the whole difference was in the first 25 years. There were no differences between Economics and Physics in the last 25 years. Maybe the explanation for these observations is that when something is new there is a need to mention it, but when it is uncontroversial and established there is not the same need to mention it.

2.6   CONCLUSION

The hypothesis formulated in the beginning was that Economics studies an object with a chaos-like structure while large parts of Physics do not. From this hypothesis followed a number of implications about what should be found in the Nobel Prize motivations. The words *framework* and *analysis* should be more common in the Economics motivations and the words *describe* and *confirm* should be common in the Physics motivations. Reference to statistics should also be more common in Economics. Statements about laurates having found exact laws and stable quantities should be found in Physics and not in Economics, and finally that Mathematics should be used in different ways.

The empirical investigation of the motivations for awarding the Nobel Prize gave support to all these implications. It is well known that many theories may be consistent with a certain set of observations. Maybe there are some other explanations for the differences observed in the Nobel Prize motivations for Economics and Physics, instead of a difference in the type of object that they study. Thinking in Bayesian terms – which I like to do – the posterior probability of the hypothesis depend on how likely the observations are if the hypothesis actually is false. Is it probable that we would find the differences in the motivations above if Economics and Physics studied the same type of object?

At least for me, it is difficult to see what a credible competing hypothesis could be, and in the rest of the book I will therefore assume that the hypothesis that Economics study a chaos-theoretic object is correct.

3. What economists do: (1) path-breaking contributions

3.1 INTRODUCTION

In this and the following chapter I look closer at what economist do and claim to accomplish. In this chapter the aim is to focus on what are seen as more path-breaking contributions while the next chapter focuses on more ordinary scientific activities and contributions. This chapter is based on the motivations given by the Nobel Prize committee for awarding the prize in Economics while the next chapter is based on an analysis of articles in *American Economic Review*. As described in the appendix, the method was to go through the motivations and collect formulations about what type of contribution the laurate had done and then to try to find a pattern and systematize these formulations. Unless otherwise stated the quotations in the tables below comes from the official motivation published by the Nobel Prize committee.

3.2 IMPORTANT CONTRIBUTIONS: AN OVERVIEW

It was found that the contributions of the Nobel laureates in Economics could be divided into six distinct categories.

First, several of the early prizes were given to economists who laid the foundation for a new way of doing economics, where mathematical modelling was an integral part of theorizing and where econometric analysis was the core empirical method.

The second type of contribution was methodological – developing the basic methods further, but in two cases for adding a new method to the basic toolkit: laboratory experiments and field experiments.

The third type of contribution is called "Crossing the border of the research field", and here there are both economists who used the economic research strategy outside the traditional areas of economic studies, and researchers that imported ideas from other fields.

The largest number of laureates belongs to a fourth category, where they have made contributions to specific fields, for example growth theory or financial economics, typically by presenting new theories about determining factors or about relations between factors.

A small group of winners belong to a fifth type, where the contribution primarily has been to develop practically useful tools, for example linear programming, or ways to calculate the national income in a consistent way.

The sixth and final group includes contributions that do not (primarily) question fundamental assumptions or existing research strategies but develop what can be called a new perspective and present new ideas that are described as having affected the whole of economics or at least large parts of economics. In the motivations for awarding the Nobel Prize, four cases could be found where such formulations were used. I have chosen to call these ideas and contributions "mini-revolutions".

In order to make it clearer what the prize-winner has done, I have, in the following tables, included a short text for each winner.

3.3   TYPE 1: FOUNDERS OF A NEW PARADIGM

When the first Nobel Prize for economics was awarded in 1969, the presentation speech started with the following words:

> In the past forty years, economic science has developed increasingly in the direction of a mathematical specification and statistical quantification of economic contexts.

In the motivations of the first three Nobel Prizes, it was underlined that the winning economists had been important for creating what could be called a new paradigm in economics, with mathematical modelling in theoretical economics, and econometric estimates and statistical hypothesis testing in empirical economics: see Table 3.1. The figure in parentheses after the laureate's name indicates that the person has made several types of contributions and is also included in further categories below. The figure (1) simply means that the current category is first category that the laurate has been included in. The abbreviation SJE means that the quote is from the article in the *Scandinavian Journal of Economics* where the contribution of the laurate is described – see the Appendix for a description of the different type of material that are published about the Nobel Prize winners.

Table 3.1   *Founders of a new paradigm*

Year/name	Contribution (from motivations)
1969 Frisch/Tinbergen (1)	Their aim has been to lend economic theory mathematical stringency, and to render it in a form that permits empirical quantification and a statistical testing of hypotheses. One essential object has been to get away from the vague, more "literary" type of economics.
1970 Samuelson (1)	Generally speaking, Samuelson's contribution has been that, more than any other contemporary economist, he has contributed to raising the general analytical and methodological level in economic science.
1971 Hicks/Arrow (1)	Hicks used traditional differential analysis as a mathematical tool. When later more modern mathematical methods began to be introduced into economics, Arrow used them to study the properties of general equilibrium systems. SJE: Hicks' contribution consists in logic and power in the methods. (Baumol 1972, p. 524)

It should be mentioned that even though the strategies used by these early Nobel Prize winners were seen as a clear break with the past, there was of course also continuity. The following quotation from Marchionni (2013, p. 342) who discusses the paradigm in economics was probably true both before and after the revolution described above: "As is well known, in economics a good explanation is commonly held to be one that shows how the phenomenon to be explained results from the actions and interactions of rational agents".

3.4   TYPE 2: DEVELOPMENT OF SCIENTIFIC METHODS

3.4.1   Development of Econometrics/Econometric Modelling

Eight Nobel Prizes have been categorized as primarily given for further development of econometric techniques, but it should be observed that several of these winning economists also have contributed to the development of the substantive theories that are evaluated by their new methods. Lucas, who is included below, has, for example, also been included as contributing to macroeconomics, and it could be argued that Klein and Sargent/Sims also should be included in the macroeconomics category. In the Information to the public published when Sargent and Sims were awarded the Nobel Prize in 2011, one can for example read: "Some of Sargent's contributions were solely methodological, although he has also applied the new methods in highly influential empirical research" (p. 3). The impression from the motivation is however that the methodological contributions were more important and therefore only they are included here.

When the prize has been shared by several people, the people involved have sometimes been individually assigned to different types of contributions. Hansen is an example of this, as his contribution is explicitly described as having developed the statistical tools necessary for testing the other laureates' theories (Fama and Shiller).

Table 3.2   Developers of econometric methods and models

Year/name	Contribution (from motivations)
1980 Klein	For the creation of econometric models and the application to the analysis of economic fluctuations and economic policies.
1989 Haavelmo	For his clarification of the probability theory foundations of econometrics and his analyses of simultaneous economic structures.
1995 Lucas (1)	Lucas's pioneering work has created an entirely new field of econometrics, known as rational expectations econometrics.
2000 Heckman/MacFadden	Heckman: for his development of theory and methods for analyzing selective samples. McFadden: for his development of theory and methods for analyzing discrete choice.
2003 Engle/Granger	Engle: for methods of analyzing economic time series with time-varying volatility (ARCH). Granger: for methods of analyzing economic time series with common trends.
2011 Sargent/Sims	Have developed methods for answering questions regarding the causal relationship between economic policy and different macroeconomic variables such as GDP, inflation, employment and investments.
2013 Hansen	Hansen developed a statistical method that is particularly well suited to testing rational theories of asset pricing.
2021 Angrist & Imbens	For their methodological contributions to the analysis of causal relationships.

3.4.2   Development of Mathematical Modelling

There are two prizes that clearly belong to this category: Debreu in 1983 and Allais in 1988. For several of the game theoretical contributions, it also seems correct to say that a very important part of their work was to develop the mathematical tools necessary, and that they saw themselves primarily as mathematicians. In Table 3.3, Nash has been included, but it could be argued that one should also include Aumann (laureate 2005) and Shapley (laureate 2012) in this category, but I have chosen to classify them only as contributing to the mini-revolution caused by game-theory.

Both Debreu and Allais used their mathematical skills to develop micro-economic theory (general equilibrium theory), but in the motivations their substantive contributions to the theory were seen as less important than the development of more stringent mathematical methods.

Table 3.3   Developers of mathematical modelling

Year/name	Contribution (from motivations)
1983 Debreu	Gerard Debreu symbolizes the use of a new mathematical apparatus. SJE: At an even more basic level, the axiomatic approach used by Debreu and his colleagues has been adopted by the profession as a standard mode of economic analysis. (Varian 1984, p. 5)
1988 Allais	The foremost contribution of Maurice Allais was made in the 1940s when he continued to develop Walras's and Pareto's work by providing increasingly rigorous mathematical formulations of market equilibrium and the efficiency properties of markets.
1994 Nash (1)	For pioneering analysis of equilibria in the theory of non-cooperative games.

3.4.3   Introduction and Development of New Empirical Methods

In the original paradigm, empirical studies used "hard data" and econometric methods. During the studied period, laboratory experiments have become an accepted method in economics. As well as the prize to Smith in 2002, the prize to Roth is also included here, as he is also described as important in the development of laboratory experiments. The quotation in Table 3.4 for Roth comes from the Advanced Information.

The prize in 2019 to Banerjee, Duflo and Kremer was motivated both by their use of field experiments and their contributions to development economics.

Table 3.4   Introducers of new (empirical) methods

Year/name	Contribution (from motivations)
2002 Smith	For having established laboratory experiments as a tool in empirical economic analysis, especially in the study of alternative market mechanisms
2012 Roth (1)	Controlled laboratory experiments are frequently used in the field of market design. Vernon Smith shared the 2002 Prize for his work in experimental economics. Alvin Roth is another major contributor in this area.
2019 Banerjee, Duflo & Kremer (1)	For their experimental approach to alleviating global poverty

3.5 TYPE 3: CROSSING THE BORDERS OF THE RESEARCH FIELD

3.5.1 Applying the Paradigm Outside the Core Area

When there is an established research tradition in a scientific field, one type of contribution is to show that the same framework can be applied to non-standard issues, typically questions that traditionally have been seen as belonging to another scientific field. The examples here concern using the economic framework for analysing politics, family formation, crime and economic history. Five prizes fit into this category and Becker is in one of the texts called "one of the most outstanding of the imperialists" (Sandmo 1993, p 7): see Table 3.5.

Table 3.5   Using the framework of Economics outside the core area

Year/name	Contribution (from motivations)
1982 Stigler	For his seminal studies of industrial structures, functioning of markets and causes and effects of public regulation. SJE: But one can argue that his work on regulation has been the most important. (Schmalensee 1983, p. 83)
1986 Buchanan	The *first* contribution from Public Choice theory, that probably is the most widely known outside the academic world, is the extension and use of traditional economic micro-theory in the studies of the political system, the public administration, and interest organizations.
1992 Becker	For having extended the domain of microeconomic analysis to a wide range of human behaviour and interaction, including nonmarket behaviour.
1993 Fogel & North	For having renewed research in economic history by applying economic theory and quantitative methods in order to explain economic and institutional change

3.5.2 Integrating Knowledge from Other Fields into Economic Analysis

If the category above can be seen as economic imperialism, the current category is the opposite. Here, the contribution is to take knowledge from other fields and integrate it into economic analysis. This can concern knowledge from political science, business administration, philosophy, sociology and/or psychology. Five prizes fit into this category: see Table 3.6.

Table 3.6   Integrating knowledge from other areas into Economics

Year/name	Contribution (from motivations)
1974 Myrdal & Hayek	For their penetrating analysis of the interdependence of economic, social and institutional phenomena
1981 Simon	He starts from the psychology of learning, with its less complicated rules of choice and its more moderate demands on the memory and the calculating capacity of the decision-maker. SJE: Surely, if ever there was a case where interdisciplinary strengths have borne fruit in economics, this is it. (Baumol 1979, p. 82)
1998 Sen (1)	By combining tools from economics and philosophy, he has restored an ethical dimension to the discussion of vital economic problems.
2002 Kahneman	For having integrated insights from psychological research into economic science, especially concerning human judgment and decision-making under uncertainty
2017 Thaler	has incorporated psychologically realistic assumptions into analyses of economic decision-making.

There are a few other cases where similar formulations have been found, but then not as a main contribution. In the Advanced Information in 2001 concerning Akerlof it is, for example, written that he "has been innovative in enriching economic theory with insights from sociology and social anthropology" (p. 4).

3.6   TYPE 4: DEVELOPING KNOWLEDGE WITHIN SPECIFIC FIELDS

In this category, the prize motivations refer to a specific part of economics, and that the laureate has made important substantial contributions to this field, typically presenting new theories about what can explain a certain phenomenon. This is the most common type of contribution by the economists, and I have divided these contributions in line with general economic areas.

3.6.1   Business Cycles and Stabilization Policy

As mentioned above, several persons won the prize for work on the intersection between the development of econometric methods and macroeconomic theory. This is clearest for Frisch/Tinbergen, Lucas and Sargent/Sims. Tobin has been included in this category even though financial markets are mentioned in the motivation for his prize. His integration of financial markets into macroeconomic theory is judged to be more important than his contribution to financial theory as such (see for example Purvis 1982, p. 68).

Table 3.7   Business cycles and stabilization policies

Year/name	Contribution (from motivations)
1969 Frisch/Tinbergen (2)	For having developed and applied dynamic models for the analysis of economic processes. Constructed theories for stabilization policy and long-term economic planning.
1976 Friedman	For his achievements in the fields of consumption analysis, monetary history and theory and for his demonstration of the complexity of stabilization policy
1981 Tobin	For his analysis of financial markets and their relations to expenditure decisions, employment, production and prices.
1995 Lucas (2)	For having developed and applied the hypothesis of rational expectations, and thereby having transformed macroeconomic analysis and deepened our understanding of economic policy.
1999 Mundell (1)	For his analysis of monetary and fiscal policy under different exchange rate regimes and his analysis of optimum currency areas.
2004 Kydland/Prescott	For their contributions to dynamic macroeconomics: the time consistency of economic policy and the driving forces behind business cycles.
2006 Phelps (2)	For his analysis of intertemporal tradeoffs in macroeconomic policy.
2011 Sargent/Sims (2)	For their empirical research on cause and effect in the macroeconomy.
2018 Nordhaus	For integrating climate change into long-run macroeconomic analysis

3.6.2   Microeconomics

Microeconomics here covers areas that are included in standard (older) micro-economic textbooks, and therefore welfare economics and general equilibrium theory are counted as part of microeconomics. Contributions focusing on how specific markets work, or can be made to work, and how prices are determined in specific markets are also included, which is why mechanism design theory, asset price theories and contributions concerning the effects of regulations also are included: see Table 3.8.

Table 3.8   Microeconomics

Year/name	Contribution (from motivations)
1969 Samuelson (2)	Samuelson's theory of "revealed preferences", a theory which has provided economists with considerably improved tools for analysis in consumption theory. A third area where Samuelson has made great contributions is general equilibrium theory.
1972 Hicks/Arrow (2)	Pioneering contributions to general economic equilibrium theory and welfare theory.
1978 Simon (2)	What is new in Simon's ideas is, most of all, that he rejects the assumption made in the classic theory of the firm of an omniscient, rational, profit-maximizing entrepreneur.
1998 Sen (2)	For his contributions to welfare economics.
2007 Hurwicz/Maskin/Meyerson	For having laid the foundations of mechanism design theory.
2010 Diamond/Mortensen/Pissarides	For their analysis of markets with search frictions.
2013 Fama/Shiller	For their empirical analysis of asset prices. Eugene Fama and several collaborators demonstrated that stock prices are extremely difficult to predict in the short run, and that new information is very quickly incorporated into prices. Shiller discovered there was significant predictability over longer time horizons… stimulated the emergence of a new research field, behavioral finance.
2014 Tirole	For his analysis of market power and regulation
2020 Milgrom/Wilson	For improvements to auction theory and inventions of new auction formats.
2021 Card	For his empirical contributions to labour economics.

3.6.3   Growth and Development Economics

Of the four prizes included here (see Table 3.9), the most problematic case is Deaton, as he is one of the cases where the prize is given for several specific contributions in different areas of economics. One could also have included him in the microeconomics category for his contribution to consumption studies.

Table 3.9   *Growth and development economics*

Year/name	Contribution (from motivations)
1971 Kuznets	For his empirically founded interpretation of economic growth.
1979 Schultz/Lewis	For their pioneering research into economic development research with particular consideration of the problems of developing countries.
1987 Solow	Solow has created a theoretical framework which can be used in discussing the factors which lie behind economic growth in both quantitative and theoretical terms.
2015 Deaton	For his analysis of consumption, poverty, and welfare: Deaton helped transform development economics from a largely theoretical field based on crude macro data, to a field dominated by empirical research based on high-quality micro data.
2017 Romer	For integrating technological innovations into long-run macroeconomic analysis.
2019 Banerjee, Duflo & Kremer (2)	For their experimental approach to alleviating global poverty.

For some other prize winners, contributions to growth theory and development economics are mentioned as a secondary contribution (Stiglitz, Phelps and Krugman), but it seems obvious that their other contributions are more important. Fogel/North were classified as contributing by using the economic approach outside traditional areas, but by doing this they also contributed to growth and development economics, and therefore they could also have been included in the current category.

3.6.4   International Economics

There is an overlap between macroeconomics and international economics, as Mundell in particular illustrates, and he has therefore been included in both categories. Three prizes are included in this group, see Table 3.10.

Table 3.10   *International economics*

Year/name	Contribution (from motivations)
1977 Ohlin/Meade	For their pathbreaking contribution to the theory of international trade and international capital movements.
1999 Mundell (2)	For his analysis of monetary and fiscal policy under different exchange rate regimes and his analysis of optimum currency areas.
2008 Krugman	For his analysis of trade patterns and location of economic activity.

It could also be argued that Samuelson should have been added here, as the Stolper-Samuelson theorem is mentioned in the motivations, but it was judged that the other contributions were more important.

3.6.5   Financial Economics

Studies of financial markets are mentioned especially in three motivations (see Table 3.11), but the borderline to microeconomics is far from clear. Should Fama have been included in this category instead, or should all of the laureates below be included in Microeconomics? The formulations in the motivations have in the end determined the categorization and, for the prizes in Table 3.11, contributions to financial economics were underlined in the motivations.

Table 3.11   Financial economics

Year/name	Contribution (from motivations)
1985 Modigliani	For his pioneering analyses of saving and of financial markets.
1990 Markowitz/Miller/Sharpe	Markowitz: awarded the Prize for having developed the theory of portfolio choice. Miller: for his contributions to the theory of price formation for financial assets. Sharpe: for his fundamental contributions to the theory of corporate finance.
1997 Merton/Scholes (1)	Developed a pioneering formula for the valuation of stock options.
2022 Bernanke, Diamond & Dybvig	For research on banks and financial crises.

3.7   TYPE 5: NEW PRACTICAL TOOLS

There are three early prizes that do not fit neatly into any of the categories above, and they have in common that these laureates developed more practical tools that are useful in various contexts. This is the case for input–output analysis, linear programming (activity analysis) and the development of a system for national accounts.

For three later prizes, it is especially underlined in the motivations that the laureate developed methods that are used in practice, to a large extent, on specific markets. This concerns Vickrey and the design of auctions, Roth and the design of matching models and Black/Scholes for their option pricing formula. They have therefore been included here (see Table 3.12), even if they also are included in other categories.

Table 3.12   New practical tools

Year/name	Contribution (from motivations)
1973 Leontieff	For the development of the input–output method and for its application to important economic problems.
1975 Kantorovitch/Koopmans	Early in his research, Professor Kantorovich applied the analytical technique of linear programming to demonstrate how economic planning in his country could be improved. Professor Koopmans, for his part, has shown for instance that on the basis of certain efficiency criteria, it is possible directly to make important deductions concerning optimum price systems.
1984 Stone	For having made fundamental contributions to the development of systems of national accounts and hence greatly improved the basis for empirical economic analysis.
1996 Vickrey (2)	His endeavors have provided the basis for a lively field of research which, more recently, has also been extended to practical applications such as auctions of treasury bonds and band spectrum licenses.
1997 Merton/Scholes (2)	Thousands of traders and investors now use this formula every day to value stock options in markets throughout the world.
2012 Roth (2)	Helped redesign existing institutions for matching new doctors with hospitals, students with schools, and organ donors with patients.

There are of course numerous laureates whose contributions have influenced economic policy. For example, in the motivation of the prize to McFadden, his extensive applications of his own methods are mentioned, especially for the San Francisco BART system. In the cases included in Table 3.12, the practical applications were relatively more important in the motivations than for others. In the speech to Hart & Holmstrom (2016) for their contribution to contract theory it was said: "Your research is an outstanding example of practically useful theory, in the best sense of the term". Examples of practical use can also be found in the motivation of the prize to Thaler (2017), where it is said that his theory about nudging had been used in several countries in the design of pension schemes. Practical use is also mentioned in the prize motivation for Banerjee, Duflo & Kremer (2019) and for Milgrom & Wilson (2020).

3.8   TYPE 6: INTRODUCING AND DEVELOPING NEW PERSPECTIVES AFFECTING ECONOMICS AS A WHOLE

In four cases, laureates are described as having come up with ideas that in the motivations are claimed to have affected not only a specific part of economics, but economics as a whole. An important aspect of these motivations is, however, that their contribution is not described as questioning an existing paradigm or as launching a new paradigm. Even though they have, so to speak, changed the way economist look at economic phenomena, their work is still consistent with central assumptions and research strategies that are established. The researchers have found an aspect that had been neglected in earlier economic theories and in economic research. These cases have here been called *mini-revolutions* in Economics, and four such mini-revolutions were found in the material during the period covered. The mini-revolutions are presented in chronological order based on the year when the first prize in each area were given. It should be underlined that the classification is only based on what is claimed in the motivations for awarding the Nobel Prize, and not on an empirical study about how these different researchers have actually influenced economics.

3.8.1   (1) Transaction Cost and Making the Institutional Structure Endogenous

In traditional macro- and microeconomics, the institutional structure is more or less taken for granted, but the new transactions cost perspective opens up questions about why there is a certain institutional structure, including certain types of contracts. This is important in all economic areas. In the press release when Coase was awarded the prize one can read:

> Coase also demonstrated that the power and precision of analysis may be enhanced if it is carried out in terms of rights to use goods and factors of production instead of the goods and factors themselves ... Coase may be said to have identified a new set of "elementary particles" in the economic system.

Coase's ideas were then developed by Ostrom and Williamson who won the prize in 2009 (see Table 3.13). In that press release one can read: "Over the last three decades these seminal contributions have advanced economic governance research from the fringe to the forefront of scientific attention".

Table 3.13   *Introducing and developing a new perspective: (1)*
                              Transaction cost analysis

Year/name	Contribution (from motivations)
1991 Coase	For his discovery and clarification of the significance of transaction costs and property rights for the institutional structure and functioning of the economy.
2009 Ostrom/Williamsson	Ostrom: for her analysis of economic governance, especially the commons. Williamson for his analysis of economic governance, especially the boundaries of the firm.
2016 Hart/Holmstrom	For their contributions to contract theory: This year's laureates have developed contract theory, a comprehensive framework for analysing many diverse issues in contractual design

3.8.2   (2) Game Theory and Strategic Behaviour

The second new perspective was introduced by game theory (see Table 3.14). Instead of seeing the economy as driven by anonymous market forces, game theory says that one should assume that actors base their decisions on expectations about what others will do. Besides the classical example of oligopolistic markets, in the motivations it is also mentioned that game theory can help us understand political decision makers and central bankers. Schelling is described as having "set forth his vision of game theory as a unifying framework for the social sciences". In the article about Nash/Harsanyi/Selten it is stated that game-theoretic concepts, terminology, and modes of analysis have come to dominate most areas of economics, and that it is the foundation of major parts of modern economics (Van Damme & Weibull 1995, p. 38).

*Table 3.14   Introducing and developing a new perspective: (2) Game
                 theory and strategic behaviour*

Year/name	Contribution (from motivations)
1994 Nash/Selten/Harsanyi (2)	In particular, non-cooperative game theory, i.e., the branch of game theory which excludes binding agreements, has had great impact on economic research. The principal aspect of this theory is the concept of equilibrium, which is used to make predictions about the outcome of strategic interaction. John F. Nash, Reinhard Selten and John C. Harsanyi are three researchers who have made eminent contributions to this type of equilibrium analysis.
2005 Schelling/Aumann (2)	For having enhanced our understanding of conflict and cooperation through game-theory analysis. Aumann was the first to conduct a full-fledged formal analysis of so-called infinitely repeated games.
2012 Shapley	Used so-called cooperative game theory to study and compare different matching methods.

3.8.3   (3) Rational Expectations

The third of the new perspectives was the theory of rational expectations, which can be seen as having two parts: that expectations are very important for behaviour, and that people are rational when they form these expectations, i.e. use all available information and the best available theories. In the motivations of the prizes to Lucas and Phelps, their role for introducing this new perspective is underlined. In the motivations it is stated that this is not only relevant for macroeconomic policy, but also for asset pricing and for various microeconomic models, e.g. models based on game theory: see Table 3.15.

*Table 3.15   Introducing and developing a new perspective: (3) Rational
                 expectations*

Year/name	Contribution (from motivations)
1995 Lucas (3)	For having developed and applied the hypothesis of rational expectations.
2006 Phelps (2)	He developed a new theory of unemployment and inflation that highlighted the role of inflation expectations as well as information problems in the labour market.

3.8.4   (4) Asymmetric information

The final case where it was said in the motivations that the contribution affected the whole of economics is the prizes for introducing theories about asymmetric information and moral hazard problems. In the motivations for the prize to Vickrey and Mirrlees one can read: "Incomplete and asymmetrically distributed information has fundamental consequences, particularly in the sense that an informational advantage can often be exploited strategically". It is stated that this has generated a better understanding of insurance markets, credit markets, auctions, the internal organization of firms, wage forms, tax systems, social insurance, competitive conditions, political institutions, etc. In the motivation for the prize to Akerlof, Spence and Stiglitz it is said that applications have been abundant, ranging from traditional agricultural markets to modern financial markets: see Table 3.16.

Table 3.16   Introducing and developing a new perspective: Asymmetric information

Year/name	Contribution (from motivations)
1996 Vickrey (2)/Mirrlees	For their fundamental contributions to the economic theory of incentives under asymmetric information.
2001 Akerlof/Spence/Stiglitz	During the 1970s, this year's Laureates laid the foundation for a general theory of markets with asymmetric information.

3.8.5   Other Mini-revolutions?

In Barberis's article "Richard Thaler and the rise of behavioral economics" (2018, p. 681) there is a discussion about whether behavioural aspects are now so integrated in all parts of economics that it has disappeared as a special field. Barberis thinks that this soon might be the case. The rise of behavioural economics could be seen as a fifth mini-revolution in economics, but the formulations in the Nobel Prize motivations about the new ideas' importance for all areas of economics were stronger in the four cases described above.

3.9   CONCLUDING COMMENTS

I will return to the discussion about paradigms and how economics change over time in Chapter 5, but I would like to emphasize the contributions that are called mini-revolutions above. My impression is that this phenomenon is not something that has been discussed in the methodological literature. What is special with these mini-revolutions is that they change the whole field by adding a new aspect, a new way of looking at things, but that they do not question a number of the fundamental assumptions of the dominating theories, for example assumptions about rationality. Neither do they argue explicitly for alternative methods of doing research.

The results in this chapter can also be related to the idea that Economics studies a chaos-theoretic object. First, it was clear from the presentation of the prize winners above that no economist won the Nobel Prize for finding an empirical law, which is exactly what we should expect if economists study a chaos-like object. Second, this chapter has also shown the importance of theoretical frameworks, and all the mini-revolutions above can be said to contain a new general framework for approaching economic issues and, in that way, they help us understand this chaos-theoretic object better, even if they do not contain any precise statement about relations between phenomena.

4.   What economists do: (2) contributions in "normal science"

4.1   INTRODUCTION AND OVERVIEW

This chapter is based on a study of 100 articles in *American Economic Review* from 1990 and 100 articles from 2020 (see the Appendix for details about the selection). During the first reading of these articles the question was "What have the authors done?" Of course, they had been coming up with ideas, been thinking about a number of things, discussing with colleagues and had written texts, but I was trying to identify what might be called *the core of their scientific activity*. It turned out that the articles fell rather neatly into three broad categories from this perspective.

1.   Articles where a mathematical model is presented and propositions concerning this model are proven.
2.   Articles where an empirical investigation is presented and where there is no analysis of a mathematical model. The empirical analysis can be a traditional econometric estimation or an experimental or quasi-experimental study.
3.   Articles where one can find both an analysis of a mathematical model and an empirical study.

As can be seen in Table 4.1, the share of type 1 articles fell between 1990 and 2020, while the pure empirical articles increased in number. This "empirical turn" in Economics was also found and discussed in for example Backhouse and Cherrier (2017) and Angrist et al (2017). Backhouse and Cherrier give an overview of a number of studies pointing to a larger share of applied economics over time. Angrist et al used machine learning to classify more than 100,000 published papers from 1990 to 2015 and found that the share of papers classified as empirical increased continuously and was 55 per cent in 2015.

As can be seen in Table 4.1, there is also a small group of articles that primarily aim at presenting new methods or improved versions of earlier methods, for example statistical methods.

In Sections 4.2–4.4 below, I look closer at each of these three main types of articles. Different subtypes and purposes of the articles are investigated. In

Table 4.1   Types of articles published

Type of article	1990 number and percentage	2020 number and percentage	Percentage 1990 excluding types 4 and 5	Percentage 2020 excluding types 4 and 5
1. Proofs of properties in mathematical model	57	31	59	33
2. Empirical study only	17	38	17	40
3. Both mathematical model and empirical study	23	25	24	27
4. Methodological	3	5		
5. Other	0	1		

Section 4.5, I look closer at how the authors of the different types of articles describe the contribution of their study in relation to earlier studies. Section 4.6 looks at how the conclusions from the studies were formulated. In Section 4.7 there are some comments about what the authors say about generalization of results.

If we look at the more recent Nobel Prize winners, we find that a small group of laurates have written important articles that do not belong to any of three main categories above. Examples of this are Roland Coase, Oliver Williamson and Elinor Ostrom. In Section 4.8, I discuss what the two most recent of these Nobel Prize winners have done in their scientific activity. What do their path-breaking articles contain if they does not contain any of the types of research activity that can be found in the articles from AER. Concluding comments can be found in Section 4.9, including comments about how the result is related to the idea that Economics studies a chaos-theoretic object.

4.2   TYPE 1 ARTICLES: PROVING THAT CERTAIN RELATIONS HOLD IN A MATHEMATICAL MODEL

In this first type of article, the main body of the article is the presentation of a mathematical model and proofs of various propositions concerning this model, e.g. that there is a certain relation between variables and/or that certain things occur given certain assumptions. In a few of the articles, quantified examples are presented, but no explicit empirical analysis is carried out.

When I submitted an article based on this study to a journal, one of the referees seemed rather upset by the label "Proofs of properties in mathematical models" for what the referee obviously called "theoretical studies". My ambition was, however, to focus on what the researchers actually had done and what took up most of the articles: and what they actually were doing was describing the structure of a mathematical model and proving various theorems concerning this model. The label "Proofs of properties in mathematical models" should not be seen as derogatory in any sense. After describing what the economist actually had done one can discuss what the economist had accomplished through this activity. Initially, however, a clear and neutral description of the activity is needed.

When I read philosophy in the middle of the 1970s, my professor sympathized with the ideas of the late Wittgenstein and what was called the Oxford school or Ordinary language philosophy. Ryle and Austin were leading names. One aspect of this school is a general initial scepticism towards abstract terms. Calling something a "theoretical analysis" does not, as I see it, convey much information about what is actually done and such a label should therefore be met with scepticism, unless there is a clear definition of what the term refers to.

The articles that belonged to this first category were analysed from a number of different perspectives. The first aspect concerned the aim of the analysis. What are the researchers trying to accomplish with their analysis of the mathematical model? The answer to this question was found by looking closer, primarily at the introductory section and the abstract of the articles.

Most of the Type 1 articles have, in the introduction, a reference to some kind of real-world situation or a real-world problem. The explicit aim of the studies of this subtype is to *explain* the observed situation or point to the *effect* of some observed factor. It is shown in the article that, in the presented model, a certain set of factors can explain the observed facts, or that the factor that the researcher is interested in has certain effects in the model. Conclusions are typically drawn by looking at characteristics of equilibria in the model and by comparing equilibria: what is to be explained occurs in equilibrium given certain assumptions, and the equilibrium changes in a certain way when a certain factor is changed. The factor that explains something is the assumption that is needed to make the thing to be explained occur in the model.

A second subtype of articles has a *normative* purpose, for example finding out what the optimal tax or the optimal contract are in a certain situation. Articles that are analysing "Mechanism-design problems" are included in this group. There are similarities between these normative articles and the first subtype as part of the analysis in both cases is to analyse the effects of certain factors. In the introduction in the normative papers there are also references to certain real-world situations.

A few articles are a mix of the first two subtypes as they both want to explain something and discuss what is optimal. It was not possible to classify one goal as more important than the other.

A third subtype consists of a small number of articles that started from earlier models/theories but made no reference to any real-world situation. The aim was, for example, to generalize a certain result or adapt an earlier model to cover a situation that the original model did not cover. In Table 4.2 these articles are just called "Other".

In all types of Type 1 articles, the introduction typically also says something about limitations in earlier models used to analyse the problem and why the presented research is important.

Table 4.2   Number and share of articles of the different subtypes

Type	1990 number	2020 number	1990 percentage	2020 percentage
1.1 Explain and/or show effect of	44	16	77	51
1.2 Normative	7	8	12	26
1.1+1.2 Both explain and normative	2	3	4	10
1.3 Other	4	4	7	13
Total	57	31		

The only statistically significant change between 1990 and 2020 at the 5 per cent level is that the share of articles where the aim is to explain or analyse effects has fallen between 1990 and 2020. The increase in the share of normative articles was almost significant at the 5 per cent level. These results are independent of how the articles classified as "both explain and normative" (Type 1.3) are allocated between Type 1.1 and Type 1.2. The "Other" group is too small to analyse statistically.

In Box 4.1, the abstract of one randomly selected article of the two main sub-types from 2020 is presented in order to make it easier to understand the characteristics of the different sub-types of articles.

BOX 4.1   ABSTRACTS FROM THE DIFFERENT TYPES OF MODEL-BASED ARTICLES: A RANDOM SELECTION

Article of Type 1.1: Acquiring information through peers

"We develop an endogenous network formation model, in which agents form connections to acquire information. Our model features complementarity in actions as agents care not only about accuracy of their decision-making but also about the actions of other agents. In equilibrium, the information structure is a hierarchical network, and, under weakly convex cost of forming links, the equilibrium network is core-periphery. Although agents are ex ante identical, there is ex post heterogeneity in payoffs and actions."

Article of Type 1.2: Optimal taxation with behavioural agents

"This paper develops a theory of optimal taxation with behavioral agents. We use a general framework that encompasses a wide range of biases such as misperceptions and internalities. We revisit the three pillars of optimal taxation: Ramsey (linear commodity taxation to raise revenues and redistribute), Pigou (linear commodity taxation to correct externalities), and Mirrlees (nonlinear income taxation). We show how the canonical optimal tax formulas are modified and lead to novel economic insights. We also show how to incorporate nudges in the optimal taxation framework, and jointly characterize optimal taxes and nudges."

4.3   TYPE 2 ARTICLES: "PURE" EMPIRICAL STUDY

In these articles there is "only" an empirical study and no analysis of a mathematical model. Most of these studies are concerned with the effects of an event or the effects of a policy. In a smaller group of articles, the aim is formulated in terms of what can explain something or what has been the cause of an event or development.

A first question to look at is the general design of the empirical study. The designs were divided into four groups, but the lines are not always completely clear. In a few cases several methods have been used, for example both a field experiment and a laboratory experiment. The classification below is based on what the authors treat as the main method.

The following four general designs were identified:

- Subtype 2.1: Using non-experimental data: classical cross-section or longitudinal study.
- Subtype 2.2: Laboratory experiments (randomized)
- Subtype 2.3: Field experiments (randomized).
- Subtype 2.4: Using non-experimental data, but using a "natural" experiment or a "quasi-experimental design" to simulate a real experiment, for example by using a discontinuity design.

For each design I have randomly selected one article from 2020, and the abstract for these articles are presented in Box 4.2. The abstracts should give a clearer picture of studies of the different types.

BOX 4.2   ABSTRACTS FROM DIFFERENT TYPES OF EMPIRICAL ARTICLES: A RANDOM SELECTION

Subtype 2.1: Factory productivity and the concession system of incorporation in late Imperial Russia, 1894–1908

"In Imperial Russia, incorporation required an expensive special concession, yet over 4,000 Russian firms incorporated before 1914. I identify the characteristics of incorporating firms and measure the productivity gains and growth in machine power enjoyed by corporations using newly-constructed factory-level panel data compiled from Russian factory censuses. Factories owned by corporations were larger, more productive, and more mechanized than unincorporated factories. Higher productivity factories were more likely to incorporate and, after incorporating, added machine power and became even more labor productive. Russian firms sought the corporate form's full set of advantages, not just stock markets access, to obtain scarce long-term financing."

Subtype 2.2: The dynamics of motivated beliefs

"A key question in the literature on motivated reasoning and self-deception is how motivated beliefs are sustained in the presence of feedback. In this paper, we explore dynamic motivated belief patterns after feedback. We establish that positive feedback has a persistent effect on beliefs. Negative feedback, instead, influences beliefs in the short run, but this effect fades over time. We investigate the mechanisms of this dynamic pattern, and provide evidence for an asymmetry in the recall of feedback. Finally, we establish that, in line with theoretical accounts, incentives for belief accuracy mitigate the role of motivated reasoning."

Subtype 2.3: Estimating the production function for human capital: results from a randomized controlled trial in Colombia

"We examine the channels through which a randomized early childhood intervention in Colombia led to significant gains in cognitive and socio-emotional skills among a sample of disadvantaged children aged 12 to 24 months at baseline. We estimate the determinants of parents' material and time investments in these children and evaluate the impact of the treatment on such investments. We then estimate the production functions for cognitive and socio-emotional skills. The effects of the program can be explained by increases in parental investments, emphasizing the importance of parenting interventions at an early age."

Subtype 2.4: The reach of radio: ending civil conflict through rebel demobilization

"We examine the role of FM radio in mitigating violent conflict. We collect original data on radio broadcasts encouraging defections during the Lord's Resistance Army (LRA) insurgency. This constitutes the first quantitative evaluation of an active counterinsurgency policy that encourages defections through radio messages. Exploiting random topography-driven variation in radio coverage along with panel variation at the grid-cell level, we identify the causal effect of messaging on violence. Broadcasting defection messages increases defections and reduces fatalities, violence against civilians, and clashes with security forces. Income shocks have opposing effects on both the conflict and the effectiveness of messaging."

As can be seen in Table 4.3, there is a large increase in the use of both field experiments and quasi-experimental approaches, while the share of classical regression studies and of laboratory experiments has fallen. The increase in quasi-experimental methods is statistically significant and the increase in field experiments is close to being statistically significant at the 5 per cent level.

Table 4.3   General design of the empirical studies

	1990	2020	1990 percentage	2020 percentage
2.1 Non-experimental: classical	13	20	77	53
2.2 Laboratory experiment	3	2	18	5
2.3 Field experiment	1	7	7	18
2.4 Non-experimental: quasi-experimental	0	9	0	24
Total	17	38		

Even though it is not important from the perspective of this book, it can be mentioned that around 10 per cent of the articles in both periods were studying historical periods (periods before 1990). The share of studies using data from non-western countries increased from zero in 1990 to around 35 per cent in 2020. Many of the studies using data from developing countries were, however, not studying questions that are specifically related to economic development.

4.4   TYPE 3 ARTICLES: ARTICLES WITH BOTH A MATHEMATICAL MODEL AND AN EMPIRICAL STUDY

When one looks closer at these articles it is possible to identify three different subtypes, even though there are a number of borderline cases.

Subtype 3.1

This is articles that result in a quantified model of, for example, macroeconomic relations, a certain market or a certain group of actors. First, a mathematical model is presented, and then various parameters are estimated (the model is calibrated). The quantified model is then used for explaining, predicting, policy analysis and/or welfare analysis.

Subtype 3.2

The articles in this group present a mathematical model and then derive predictions/implications from the model and then test whether these implications have empirical support.

Subtype 3.3

In these articles, the relationship between the mathematical model and the empirical study is rather weak. In some cases, the model and the empirical study are two independent ways of making the same point. In some cases, the model is followed by a more qualitative empirical study that discuss the implications of the model in relation to how certain markets/institutions are working. In a few cases the mathematical model is presented after the empirical study, for example in an appendix.

In some articles there are elements of both Types 3.1 and 3.2 and these articles have been classified as Type 3.1, as creating the quantified model dominates these articles. The shares of the different subtypes are presented in Table 4.4.

Table 4.4   *Classification of articles that include both a mathematical model and an empirical study*

	1990 (no.)	2020 (no.)	1990 (%)	2020 (%)
3.1. Quantified model	11	18	48	72
3.2. Test of implications	6	4	26	16
3.3. Weak link between model and empirical study	6	3	26	12
Total	23	25		

There is an increase in the share of quantified models, but it is not statistically significant. The only group that is big enough to analyse more in detail is category 3.1. A closer analysis of these will follow in later sections. Four randomly selected examples of articles of Type 3 from 2020 are presented in Box 4.3.

BOX 4.3   EXAMPLES OF ARTICLES OF TYPE 3

Is the cure worse than the disease? Unintended effects of payment reform in a quantity-based transfer program

"Quantity vouchers are used in redistributive programs to shield participants from price variation and alter their consumption patterns. However, because participants are insensitive to prices, vendors of program goods are incentivized to price discriminate between program and non-program customers. I study these trade-offs in the context of a reform to reduce price discrimination in the Supplemental Nutrition Program for Women, Infants, and Children (WIC), which provides a quantity voucher for nutritious foods to low-income mothers and children. The reform caused vendors to drop out, reducing program take-up. In addition, smaller vendors increased prices charged to non-WIC shoppers by 6.4 percent."

Why Special Economic Zones? Using trade policy to discriminate across importers

"Tariffs are generally assumed to depend on the product, not the identity of the importer. However, special economic zones are a common, economically important policy used worldwide to lower tariffs on selected goods for selected manufacturers. I show this is motivated by policymakers' desire to discriminate across buyers when a tax is intended to raise prices for sellers, through a mechanism distinct from existing theories of optimal taxation. Using a new dataset compiled from public records and exogenous changes in imports of intermediate goods, I find the form, composition, and size of US zones are consistent with the theory."

How well targeted are soda taxes?

"Soda taxes aim to reduce excessive sugar consumption. We assess who is most impacted by soda taxes. We estimate demand using micro longitudinal data covering on-the-go purchases, and exploit the panel dimension to estimate individual-specific preferences. We relate these preferences and counterfactual predictions to individual characteristics and show that soda taxes are relatively effective at targeting the sugar intake of the young, are less successful at targeting the intake of those with high total dietary sugar, and are unlikely to be strongly regressive especially if consumers benefit from averted internalities."

Turnover liquidity and the transmission of monetary policy

"We provide empirical evidence of a novel liquidity-based transmission mechanism through which monetary policy influences asset markets, develop a model of this mechanism, and assess the ability of the quantitative theory to match the evidence."

4.5   WHAT IS NEW ACCORDING TO THE AUTHOR?

The question investigated here is how the authors describe what their study has
added to scientific knowledge. What are the main contributions of the study?

4.5.1   Articles of Type 1

In this type of article, the author builds a mathematical model and proves relations in the model and the question is now how the authors have answered the
question: "What makes the current model better than earlier ones?"

Most articles that focus on explanation and on finding effects refer to earlier
models that have been used to study the issue or used in a broader field related
to the specific issue. The authors typically refer to some feature that is new in
their model and argue that this new feature is important from the perspective of
understanding how the world works. It can be a different behavioural assumption, different assumptions about expectations and/or different institutional
assumptions (new setting or new environment) that makes it possible to study
certain aspects in a better way than in earlier models. In some cases, this is
described as that the new model is more *general* and does not include what is
seen as *restrictive* assumptions in earlier models.

The best general description of these findings is that the new model is
more interesting than earlier models because it is believed to be more realistic
in some respect that is important in relation to the specific problem. It can
also be the case that the new model covers an observed situation that earlier
models have not covered. In some important dimensions, the new model is
more plausible than earlier ones, even though the model can be more stylized
in other dimensions. In the discussion at the end of the article about what
should be done next, it is often argued that some feature of the model may
be questionable and/or restrictive (at least for certain situations/markets) and
therefore this feature should be changed in future models. At the same time,
the authors typically argue that their result probably is robust to some other
specific changes in assumptions.

Similar observations were made concerning the normative articles of Type
1. From the perspective of scientific progress, it is common in these articles to
argue that normative conclusions in earlier studies do not hold if some assumptions are changed. The setting in the new article is believed to be more realistic
in important dimensions and therefore gives more credible recommendations
about what the optimal policy is. Examples are that the new study takes uncertainty or bounded rationality into account. Even though the new setting might
be more general and that the result can be robust to a number of changes in the

setting, the researchers are aware that the new setting also has limitations in certain respects. They sometimes point out that future research will show how robust the new results really are.

In both subtypes of articles there are sometimes comments in the final section that the article also has made a methodological contribution. The new model developed can be used to study other issues than the one studied in the article in a simpler way than what was possible with earlier models.

4.5.2   Articles of Type 2

In these "pure" empirical articles there are two dominating types of formulations about what the aim is, both in 1990 and in 2020, and these are that the aim is to *measure the effect of something* (including welfare effects) or *to explain something* (including proposing a new framework for explaining something). Both alternatives are roughly as common in both years. There are a few exceptions where the purpose is to estimate an optimal pattern.

From the perspective of scientific development there are the same types of contribution as in the Type 1 articles: either the article is said to include an aspect that has been neglected in earlier research or the articles propose to measure or explain something in a better way, in a situation where earlier measurements of effects, or earlier explanations, have been found to be problematic. As pointed out above, the starting point was in most cases both an interesting question and observed problems in earlier research.

4.5.3   Articles of Type 3

In these articles there are both a mathematical model and an empirical study. The two main purposes were also in this case to explain something and find the effect of something, typically the effect of some policy intervention. Supplementary purposes were primarily the simulation of the effects of other/ new policies. Welfare calculations were in some cases also part of the purpose independent of whether the aim was finding the effect of something or simulating the effects of alternative policies. There were no differences between the articles in 1990 and 2020. There are, as mentioned above, interactions between the purpose to study the effect of something and to explain something. Even if the focus is on explaining something, the results could have been reformulated as finding the effect of something.

Focusing on the model and progress over time, the same type of formulations could be found as for Type 1 articles. In relation to earlier models the presented model is typically described as more realistic in some respect. It can be that the new model changes specific assumptions, for example takes uncertainty, adjustment costs or behavioural aspects into account. It can also be that the model includes new links between variables or makes finer distinctions, for example includes different submarkets on a housing market or distinguishes between different types of labour skills.

4.5.4   A Comparison with the 1993 Study of Articles of Type 1

As described in the Appendix, the article "A case study of normal research in theoretical economics" was based on the study of all 36 articles that a successful (then) young (theoretical) researcher had published between 1976 and 1986. In the sections in the article describing the contribution of the studied articles, three types of formulations could be found.

Contribution 1: More realistic model-economy

This was a very common type of argument. Comments about the importance of analysing more realistic model economies could also be found in the concluding sections where future research tasks were discussed. A related type of contribution was to analyse a more general model economy, as a more general model can be realistic in some situations where a less general one is not. An example was that an earlier article was criticized for making very special assumptions about preferences. Another variant that is included in this category is when there is no general claim that the new model-economy is more realistic, but instead a claim that it is more realistic for some specific cases. An example was that, in the new article, a certain question was studied for an open economy, while earlier studies only concerned a closed economy. These types of contributions are very similar to the ones presented above for the AER-articles investigated. This is also true for the second type of contribution found in the earlier article.

Contribution 2: Better analytic techniques

In around 20 per cent of the articles studied there were also arguments saying that one contribution was the use of a better analytic technique. The analytic technique was evaluated in two dimensions: does it make the mathematical problem easier to solve (length of the proofs, etc.), and can the final formulas more easily be given an economic interpretation when the new technique is used?

Contribution 3: Better microeconomic foundations

Two properties seemed to be important in this case. The first was that the model economy should include optimizing agents (mentioned explicitly as a contribution in five of the articles). In some articles it was claimed that a weakness in earlier studies is that they include money in the utility function. This argument suggests that the description of what the agents optimize should also be psychologically reasonable, that is, include only things that give utility in a nontechnical sense. Second, an analysis was judged to be better if it includes more general-equilibrium effects, that is, more interaction between markets. This was also mentioned in five of the articles. The question why these two properties are important to include is not discussed, but my guess was that the economist saw these characteristics as rather realistic: individual behaviour is believed to be rather rational and affected by economic variables and that it is realistic to assume that markets are interrelated. If this argument is accepted, contributions of this type should be included in Type 1 contributions above: using a more realistic model.

It is interesting to note that arguments saying that a contribution of the article is that it has a better microeconomic foundation are rare in the AER-articles, both in 1990 and in 2020. One possible explanation is that when behavioural aspects are more and more integrated in Economics then the interesting question is no longer if a certain observation can be rationalized by theories of utility maximizing agents with standard preferences. The question instead becomes: which more precise behavioural assumptions can rationalize the observations that are to be explained? The contribution is then described in terms of introducing more realistic behavioural assumptions and not as giving better microeconomic foundations.

4.6   HOW CONCLUSIONS WERE FORMULATED IN THE AER-ARTICLES

The discussion in Chapter 2 about the nature of the object that economists study implies that it is interesting to look at how the conclusions in the articles are formulated and what kind of knowledge the studies have led to. Are the conclusions formulated in a way that is consistent with what can be expected if the researchers study a chaos-theoretic object?

4.6.1   Articles of Type 1

4.6.1.1 Subtype 1.1
The articles start from a real-world situation, then show what happens in a model with certain assumptions. In the conclusions the researcher typically returns to the real-world problem.

The conclusions in relation to the initial real-world problem are formulated in a number of different ways but are typically rather guarded. It is common to say that what was proved in the model *can* explain the real-world phenomena, that the analysis *suggests* or *indicates* that a certain mechanism explains the observed phenomena. The analysis of the model *throws light on* or *highlights* a certain feature that can be important for understanding the real-world phenomenon. In a few cases, somewhat stronger formulations were found, for example that the study shows that something is *probable* or *likely* given reasonable assumptions. No clear difference in formulations could be found between the articles from 1990 and those from 2020.

4.6.1.2 Subtype 1.2

There are many similarities between the normative and the positive articles, for example in how conclusions are formulated. It is typically said that the article shows that something *can* be optimal or *highlights* certain possibilities. The analysis increases our *understanding* of determinants and trade-offs. Somewhat stronger formulations could also be found in this case, for example that something *holds in a wide variety of settings* or holds for *many plausible specifications* or that the result has *profound implications for a wide range of public policies*. In the articles about optimal contracts there are sometimes references to empirical evidence indicating that features that have been shown to be optimal can be found in actual contracts in relevant markets.

4.6.2   Articles of Type 2

The following more general description can be given of the findings in the empirical articles.

The direct results of the empirical studies are that certain differences are (or are not) significant and/or that certain parameters have a certain value. This of often described in terms of *findings*: that something was *shown* or that *it is* in a certain way. In a few cases the conclusion was formulated as that the result is *consistent* with a certain theory or hypothesis.

Most articles comment on limitations and caveats related to the quality of data or assumptions in the statistical methods used. More general comments about the results have a similar terminology as in the model-based studies discussed above: The results *suggest* or *indicate* that there is a certain relation, and/or that a certain mechanism is working. The study *sheds light* on certain issues. But there are also claims that the result *seems robust to certain changes*, or that there is *strong support for something*. In a number of cases, it is also said that there are implications for policy design, but often formulated with a number of reservations.

No clear differences could be observed between formulations in the articles from 1990 and those from 2020, except that the discussions about implications often were longer in the 2020 articles, a point I will return to in a later chapter.

4.6.3   Articles of Type 3

The conclusions in these articles are described in a very similar way as in the earlier types of studies. There is a direct (quantitative) result generated by the study. The more general conclusions from the study are, in a few cases, formulated as that the results are *consistent with the model*. There were however also stronger formulations, for example that the results *strongly support a certain hypothesis*, or that something is shown to be *crucial for understanding and predicting*, or that *substantial gains can be made* by changing policy. It was, however, more common with weaker claims of the type that we met above, for example that the study *suggests* or *indicates* that a certain factor is important and that some factors or links *deserve more attention* or *should not be neglected* in future studies.

4.7   COMMENTS ON GENERALIZATIONS IN THE AER-ARTICLES

A first observation from the studied articles is that external validity, and whether the results can be generalized or not, is very seldom discussed explicitly, but there are typically discussions about reliability and robustness. The issue of external validity has in recent methodological debates been discussed by, for example, Khosrowi (2019, 2021) and Favereau and Nagatsu (2020). Favereau and Nagatsu (2020) discuss external validity in the context of randomized field experiments and introduce the term "structured speculation" as a way of describing discussions about the external validity of the experimental results.

The term *structured speculation* does however seem relevant for all the different types of articles discussed above: the structured speculation comments on various simplification and assumptions and discusses how this may affect the relevance of the result for specific situations that were explicitly covered by the research. This will be returned to more in detail in Chapter 7 where what are called "commentaries" to mathematical models are discussed.

The impression from reading the articles from the perspective of generalizations is that very similar discussions can be found in all types of articles. In the articles with proofs of relations in mathematical models, the discussion focuses on the assumptions in the model: is a rather unrealistic assumption harmless or crucial? How robust is the result to changes in assumptions? In this discussion, all kinds of materials are used by the author, from results from other studies to everyday observations of recent events.

In the articles where an econometric estimation is the central component, the discussions about robustness focus more on whether the equations were correctly specified and on the quality of the data. Similar issues are commented on in the articles where a quantified model is built.

As was seen in the presentation of the results in Section 4.6, it is in all types of articles common with very guarded final formulations, using terms such as *suggest* and *indicate* when the direct results are discussed from a broader perspective. Articles typically end with caveats and discussions of limitations.

The picture that emerges is that the researchers know that the economy is complex – that many factors interact – and that changes occur over time. Therefore, it cannot be assumed that a relation shown in a specific model or observed in one place (market, region, country) at one point in time will hold in another situation. In order to make a really well-informed statement about that, a new study has to be made with different assumptions or for different places and at different times. Until this is done it is only a conjecture that the relation will hold in at least some other cases. An example of a claim is the following: "As with many microeconomic studies, it can be challenging to generalize results to other contexts. Yet, we can specify three conditions under which we can expect to find a similar effect." These conditions were the ones that was shown to be important in the model analysed.

There seems to be a difference between the 1990- and the 2020-articles in that the "structured speculations" are given more room in the later articles, and these sections are also more structured. Often there is a rather long intro-ductory section where the researchers in 2020 more explicitly position their research in relation to different research areas, and also a more systematic discussion about the implications of their results for different research fields.

4.8   OTHER KINDS OF (IMPORTANT) ARTICLES: EXAMPLES FROM NOBEL PRIZE WINNERS

The picture that emerges from the sections above is that economists in their research do four different things: (1) build and analyse mathematical models, (2) do econometric analysis, (3) carry out field experiments, and (4) carry out laboratory experiments. But there have been successful economists who have not done any of these things, or at least only done them as a small part of their research. Returning the list of Nobel Prize winners, the two most recent economists who (primarily) have done other things are Oliver Williamson and Eleonor Ostrom (Nobel Prize winners 2009). In order to understand what one can do other than the four things above, I have looked closer at a few of the articles that these researchers have written that are mentioned in the Nobel Prize motivations as their most important works. The question that I focused on was what they actually had done in their research.

Williamson

I have looked at the articles "The vertical integration of production: Market failure considerations" (Williamson 1971) and "Franchise bidding for natural monopolies – in general and with respect to CATV" (Williamson 1976).

Both articles start with a description of the established view. In the first article, the established view was that vertical integration only can increase efficiency if there are technological dependencies. In the second article, the established view was that efficiency can be reached by using rather simple forms of franchise bidding. The counterhypothesis is that these established views are false and that the earlier authors had not analysed the situation in detail and had not taken transaction costs into account. They are in the articles criticized for having neglected to carry out a detailed "microanalytic examination".

The strategy in the vertical integration article is to describe two different types of contracts that can be used instead of vertical integration and point out that both these types of contracts have a number of problematic features. The articles could easily have been structured as a pro-and-con analysis where problems are pointed out, possible counterarguments/solutions are presented and problems in these counterarguments pointed out. The conclusion is primarily that the established view is too simplified and that there can be situations where vertical integration is efficient because it reduces transaction costs.

It is interesting to ask what kind of information is used to reach this conclusion. In the vertical integration article, no empirical study is presented but this is done in the franchise bidding article. In that article, a case study is presented to show that the kind of potential problems that were identified in the general discussion actually occur in practice. The case study is presented to make the general claims more credible.

Two other kinds of information are also used to strengthen the cases presented. The first is in reference to other literature – for example a few books on management problems. Even though it is not clear in Williamson's articles what these other authors have done, the general impression is that these books are written by persons with more direct knowledge about management problems. The fact that they refer to a certain type of problem is therefore seen as evidence that these problems actually exist.

The second type of reference in the article is to what the author sees as well-known facts that anyone with experience of working in a company or organization, or from participation in negotiations, will recognize. An example is the risk for opportunistic behaviour when there is uncertainty and information problems.

In the final section of the article about vertical integration it is said that more information about such internal processes is needed in order to draw more definitive conclusions about whether vertical integration is the most efficient alternative or not in a specific situation. The main point is, in both cases, that the dominant view is problematic and that lower transaction costs can make vertical integration more efficient than realistic alternatives.

Ostrom

I have looked at the articles "Covenants with and without a sword: Self-governance is possible" (Ostrom, Walker & Gardner 1992) and "Collective action and the evolution of social norms" (Ostrom 2000). Like Williamson, Ostrom starts from an established view: that free-rider problems make it impossible for a group of individuals to manage common resources without some kind of "state" that will uphold rules and punish free-riders. She questions this view and uses three kinds of arguments, as well as some references to everyday observations.

The first is to refer to certain game-theoretic arguments, and even though Ostrom does not build any mathematical models herself, she uses results from analyses of repeated games to argue that cooperation can be maintained given certain assumptions.

The second type of argument is to refer to carefully designed common-pool laboratory experiments that include both communication possibilities and that an individual can punish a participant who does not contribute to the common pool.

These two ways of arguing are in line with the type of studies that were found in the AER-material, but this is not true for a third type of argument. This third kind of evidence, which Ostrom seems to see as the strongest argument for her view, is a number of rather detailed case studies.

She, and other researchers, have observed a number of common pool resources that actually are managed reasonably efficiently without an external policing agency. Based on a number of case studies Ostrom formulates a hypothesis/theory about "design criteria" that can lead to a decentralized efficient management of a common resource. The case studies indicate that if these design criteria are followed then the probability of getting efficient decentralized management increases. The laboratory experiments point in the same direction.

In the same way as Williamson, Ostrom is relatively guarded in her general conclusions and focuses on the "negative" conclusions: that there are serious weaknesses in the simplified established views on the management of common resources.

4.9 CONCLUDING COMMENTS

In their research today economists do one of the following four things:

- Build mathematical models and analyse relations in these models.
- Use non-experimental data and statistical methods to draw conclusions about relations between factors, for example effects of events and policies.
- Use laboratory experiments to investigate relations.
- Use field experiments to investigate relations.

Between 1990 and 2020 the main change was that the first group decreased and the second increased in the AER-articles. In the Nobel Prize material, there were also a few examples where researchers had used case-studies to make their claims credible.

The primary aim of all types of studies is to understand how the world works and this is, of course, in line with what could be called a common-sense view of science.

The most common argument in the first type of article for why the new study is better than older studies is that the new model has incorporated some factor, or made some assumption, that is more realistic in some respect compared with earlier studies. The same holds for articles that both include a mathematical model and an empirical study. In the empirical articles, the contribution is either using new data or a new method or both – or that it measures something that has not been measured before.

I argued in Chapter 2 that Economics studies a chaos-theoretic object, and from that perspective it is not surprising that the conclusions in all kinds of studies are rather guarded. It is, for example, common to have formulations saying that the study indicates or suggests that something that earlier studies had neglected is important for understanding a certain phenomenon. It was also found that generalization of the result seldom is discussed – which is also what should be expected if there are no simple stable relations. The studies do, however, contribute more generally in the sense that they can make future studies of new situations better because they point out factors that should be taken into account. The studies presented in the articles can also use improved methods that other researchers can use in the future when studying the relations in new contexts or other relations. In the 2020 articles, there are longer and more systematic discussions about how the results should be interpreted in relation to results from earlier studies and what can make it more probable that the results also hold in other contexts.

This chapter is called "What economists do" but the focus has so far been on what they do in their research that leads to articles being published in scientific journals. It should not be forgotten that economists/scientists also do a lot of other things besides writing such articles, for example:

- They write textbooks.
- They write chapters in books, for example in the very large number of "Handbooks" that are available.
- They write books for a broader audience.
- They write columns in newspapers or in journals targeting a broader audience.
- They act as formal or informal advisors for political parties, politicians, and companies, for example they participate in temporary government committees or sit on company boards.
- They are expert-witnesses in court cases.
- They participate in committees that evaluates and ranks research grant applications or applications for university positions.

And last but not least: most researchers also teach in university courses and supervise students at different levels.

5. How Economics develops over time: Kuhn versus Laudan

5.1 INTRODUCTION

In this shorter chapter I will investigate whether the material from the Nobel Prize committee motivations for awarding the prize can be used to test different theories about how science develops over time. There is an enormous literature in this area, but I will focus on two theories: Kuhn's ideas about scientific revolutions and Laudan's theory about research traditions. In the next section, these different views are described a little more in detail while in Section 5.3 the two theories are related to the results from the study about scientific contributions as they are described in the Nobel Prize motivations. Concluding reflections can be found in Section 5.4.

5.2 THE COMPETING VIEWS

5.2.1 Kuhn

Since Kuhn's influential work The *Structure of Scientific Revolutions* (Kuhn 1970 [1962]) scientists within a certain field, at a certain point in time, have often been described as working within a specific paradigm, for example using specific methods and making certain fundamental assumptions that are not questioned. A few years later a modified version of Kuhn's theory was presented by Lakatos (Lakatos & Musgrave 1970), where scientists are described as working within a specific research program, with a "hard core" of assumptions that should not be questions and a "heuristics" that guides researchers when solving problems within the framework given by the hard core of the research programme.

Kuhn's description of how scientists work changed over time, as described in several of the articles in the book *Kuhn's Structure of Scientific Revolutions – 50 Years On* (Devlin & Bokulich 2015). This book indicates that Kuhn's theories still are relevant (see also Bird 2014). Instead of discussing science in terms of paradigms, concepts such as "disciplinary matrix", "exemplars" and "lexicons" are used in Kuhn's later works (Devlin & Bokulich 2015, p. 158).

In a disciplinary matrix there are conceptual, theoretical and methodological elements.

Dolfsma and Welch (2009) describe paradigms in terms of a "set of rules and routines" (p 1088). Solomon (2011) describes paradigms as "defining both the questions of interest and the appropriate evidence" and that a paradigm also has "a core of technical results and successful exemplars that have been extended over time" (p. 455).

From the perspective of this study, it is especially important that a paradigm or a disciplinary matrix consists of both methodological and substantive assumptions about the field under study, and that a new paradigm includes both new methodologies and new substantive assumptions. When an old paradigm is replaced with a new paradigm, both types of assumption change.

5.2.2 Laudan

Laudan (1977) uses the concept of research tradition and writes: "In brief, a research tradition provides a set of guidelines for development of specific theories" (p. 79). He criticizes both Kuhn and Lakatos with the argument that their concepts are too static and inflexible. He describes his alternative concept a little more in detail as follows (pp. 78–79).

1. Every research tradition has a number of specific theories which exemplify and partially constitute it; some of these theories will be contemporaneous, others will be temporal successors of earlier ones.
2. Every research tradition exhibits certain metaphysical and methodological commitments.
3. Each research tradition [...[goes through a number of different, detailed (and often mutually contradictory) formulations and generally has a long history.

Bird (2014, p. 50) argues, in a similar way, that:

> we can construct the following list of types of change or response to problems:
> i.   simple cumulative, no revision required;
> ii.   discovery driven by minor anomaly, requiring revision to non-paradigm beliefs;
> iii. discovery driven by minor anomaly, requiring revision to paradigm beliefs;
> iv.   minor anomaly, not solved and shelved;
> v.   serious anomaly, solved within paradigm (i.e. normal science solution);
> vi.   serious anomaly, not solved and shelved;
> vii. serious anomaly, solved with minor revision to paradigm;
> viii. serious anomaly, solved with major revision to paradigm.

The main difference between Kuhn's and Laudan/Bird's view of science is that in the Kuhnian model many components (conceptual, theoretical, methodological) change at the same time (or within a short period of time) when a revolution occurs. In the Laudan/Bird model, fundamental components can be changed one by one, and thereby over time radically transform the field, as almost all of the initial components could be replaced in a stepwise way. There is in the Laudan/Bird model no short revolutionary periods where fundamental assumption and methods change almost simultaneously.

5.3 ANALYSIS OF CONTRIBUTIONS BY NOBEL LAUREATES IN RELATION TO MODELS OF SCIENTIFIC CHANGE

5.3.1 Kuhn

If we look at the development of Economics from the perspective of Kuhn's theory, most of the contributions fit nicely into what could be called *normal-scientific development* within a given paradigm. This is true for the following types of contribution that were described in Chapter 3:

• Development of mathematical and empirical methods.
• Extending the reach of paradigm.
• New theories within a specific field that does not question the underlying general assumptions.
• New practical tools based on the paradigm.

A number of early laurates got the prize with the motivation that they had laid the foundation for what could be described as a *new economic paradigm* where mathematical modelling and econometric analysis were the core methods. If a scientific revolution is a change where both methods and the content of theories change, this described change in Economics should not be called a scientific revolution as there were no major changes in the underlying theories. Microeconomic theory with assumptions of utility-maximising consumers and profit-maximizing companies did not change and neither did the main content of theories about how markets with various degrees of competition work.

The *mini-revolutions* described in Chapter 3 – for example the introduction of game theory and theories about asymmetric information – can be described neither in terms of creating a new paradigm nor as making a normal-scientific contribution. As these mini-revolutions do not change the fundamental assumptions of rationality and do not argue for changing the methods used, they can hardly be called the introduction of a new paradigm. On the other hand, the contributions were far-reaching and were claimed to have larger effects than the typical normal-scientific contribution has.

There are a number of laureates that in one way or another challenge, or at least do not follow, core features of the dominating paradigm. These researchers can be divided into four groups.

1. *Laureates that do not follow the core methods*: During the last 25 years, the most obvious examples are Coase (in 1991) and Ostrom/Williamson (in 2009), that neither build mathematical models nor carry out econometric studies. These laureates have, however, not presented or argued for any competing methodological programme, but seem to have more of a live-and-let-live attitude. One could argue that they got the prize *despite* not following the standard methods, but they did not present any alternative systematic approach.

2. *Failed attempts to introduce different perspectives*: There are some early prize winners that got the prize for introducing ideas from other fields, and for broadening the perspective of Economics. I will not try to substantiate the claim here, but I think it is fair to say that these attempts did not change the way economists work. One case was Myrdal/Hayek who got the prize in 1974 and wanted to integrate more sociological aspects, and another one was Simon in 1981 for introducing ideas from the psychology of learning.

3. *A successful introduction of a new method*: The first Nobel Prize winner who got the prize for getting a new method accepted into the core of the paradigm was Vernon Smith and the introduction of laboratory experiments in Economics. Another example is the 2020 prize to Banerjee, Duflo & Kremer for their use of field experiments. Both methods were common in the 2020 AER-articles.

4. *A successful introduction of new basic assumptions*. In this category belong the prize to Kahneman in 2002 and Thaler in 2017. The prize in 2013 to Shiller can be seen as a follow up to the prize to Kahneman and in the Advanced information about Fama/Shiller one can read: "Many of these papers can be thought of as modifying the preference assumptions in rational-agent models, ..., which illustrates a convergence between rational and behavioral models in recent research" (p. 32). In the Advanced information about Kahneman/Smith they write: "A large and growing body of scientific work is now devoted to the empirical testing and modification of traditional postulates in economics, in particular those of unbounded rationality, pure self-interest, and complete self-control" (p. 1). As in the case of the experimental methods, there were also a considerable number of articles in the AER study where the contribution was the introduction of new behavioural assumptions.

Neither the successful innovations in methods nor the successful broadening of the fundamental behavioural assumptions fit nicely into the Kuhnian model. They are too small to be called a new paradigm: The changes in methods did not include any change in fundamental assumptions and the new fundamental assumptions could be introduced without changing the methods used. On the other hand, the changes introduced could not be called ordinary normal-scientific contributions.

5.3.2 Laudan

All the types of contribution that were difficult to fit into Kuhn's theory seem to fit nicely into Laudan's theory. This concerns the mini-revolutions, the separate introduction of new methods (laboratory experiments, field experiments) and the separate introduction of new behavioural assumptions. Laudan (1977, p. 98) writes:

> But, perhaps more often, scientists find that by introducing one of two modifications in the core assumptions of the research tradition, they can both solve the outstanding anomalies and conceptual problems and preserve the bulk of the assumptions of the research tradition intact.

5.4 CONCLUDING COMMENTS

One aspect of Kuhn's theory is, however, important to remember, and that is that new ideas initially are met with scepticism. It is therefore interesting to look at what makes a new idea accepted and there are some comments about that in the Nobel Prize texts. In the Advanced information about Kahneman and Smith it is written:

> When they appeared, Kahneman's and Smith's initial works were received with scepticism by the scientific community in economics. It took considerable time and much further research before their main ideas seriously began to penetrate the profession. (p. 21)

In order to be able to change one part of a research tradition it can be rational/ tactical to accept other parts of the research tradition. That Kahneman (and Tversky) built a mathematical model incorporating their ideas and got the article published in the very highly ranked journal *Econometrica* must have been important for getting their ideas accepted. In the case of Smith, many of his initial articles using laboratory experiments were concerned with testing whether laboratory markets behaved as markets in the established theoretical models. The main results were that the laboratory markets worked as the standard theoretical model predicted. My guess is that the initial scepticism against laboratory experiments was probably reduced when the economists saw that their theories got support from the laboratory experiment. And once the method was accepted, it was easier to use it to question the established assumptions about human behaviour.

If a research tradition is somewhat flexible and, at least after a while, incorporates new ideas and methods, a scientific revolution in the Kuhnian sense should not be expected. When various anomalies come up, and competing ideas and methods are launched that seems to be able to handle these anomalies in a better way, these ideas and methods can, after a while, be absorbed into the dominant research tradition in a way that Laudan described. A situation where a new complete paradigm is built up beside the dominant one, and then finally replaces the dominant one, will then not occur.

It could be argued that Kuhn's theory of scientific revolutions is a self-defeating theory in a world of rational researchers. When leaders in a scientific field realize that in history there have been scientific revolutions, they also realize that in order to save as much as possible of the current paradigm, it is better to accept some changes in the core elements than to fight against all such changes. The leading researchers will therefore become more interested in reforming their paradigm and opening it up to new ideas and methods in order to avoid a more radical future revolution.

This in turn changes the rational strategy for smart young researchers who are sceptical of at least some of the fundamental assumptions of the currently dominant paradigm. If they realize that it is possible to change the paradigm from within, it will be more rational to stay within the mainstream world rather than explicitly joining a group of researchers that see themselves as presenting a competing paradigm. This should also mean that the mainstream is no longer so homogeneous and rigid. Hands (2015, p. 70) describes such a development with the following words:

> John Davis, my co-editor of *The Journal of Economic Methodology*, and others, have suggested that the mainstream of disciplinary economics is no longer neoclassical: that the once dominant neoclassical framework has been replaced by a new, more pluralistic, mainstream which is more open to psychology, less individualistic, accommodates various types of path-dependencies, and allows for a much broader class of modelling strategies and tools.

6.   On theory in Economics

6.1   INTRODUCTION

The aim of this chapter is to try to cast some light on the meaning and use of theory in Economics from a number of different perspectives. There is an enormous literature on scientific theory in general and on theory in Economics. I have, however, used some well-reputed dictionaries and the definitions found in them as a starting point (Section 6.2). Section 6.3 presents the results from a study of the meaning and use of theory and hypothesis in the articles from AER. Section 6.4 discusses the relation between theory and empirical studies in these articles. Section 6.5 focuses on the meaning and use of a theoretical framework and concluding comments can be found in Section 6.6.

6.2   THEORY ACCORDING TO SOME DICTIONARIES

In the *Stanford Encyclopaedia of Philosophy* three approaches to theories are described: the *syntactic, semantic* and *pragmatic* view. I will however focus primarily on the Pragmatic View as it seems to be most relevant for Economics. It is first said that:

> The Pragmatic View recognizes that a number of assumptions about scientific theory seem to be shared by the Syntactic and Semantic Views. Both perspectives agree, very roughly, that theory is (1) explicit, (2) mathematical, (3) abstract, (4) systematic, (5) readily individualizable, (6) distinct from data and experiment, and (7) highly explanatory and predictive.

One feature of the pragmatist view is instead:

> *Pluralism*. Theory structure is plural and complex both in the sense of internal variation and of existing in many types. In other words, there is an internal pluralism of theory (and model) components (e.g., mathematical concepts, metaphors, analogies, ontological assumptions, values, natural kinds and classifications, distinctions, and policy views).

A few quotations can give a feeling for what the pragmatic view stands for:

> While these analyses [syntactic and semantic view] have advanced our under-
> standing of some formal aspects of theories and their uses, they have neglected or
> obscured those aspects dependent upon nonformal patterns in theories. Progress can
> be made in understanding scientific theories by attending to their diverse nonformal
> patterns and by identifying the axes along which such patterns might differ from
> one another.

> The crucial divide in philosophy of science, I think, is not the one between advo-
> cates of the syntactic view and advocates of the semantic view, but the one between
> those who think that philosophy of science needs a formal framework or other and
> those who think otherwise.

The pragmatist view brings theory closer to concepts such as paradigms, where
there are several components: worldview, substantive assumptions, and methodological recommendations.

In the simpler *Britannica Online Encyclopaedia* the first paragraph under
the heading "Theory" says the following:

> scientific theory, systematic ideational structure of broad scope, conceived by
> the human imagination, it encompasses a family of empirical (experiential) laws
> regarding regularities existing in objects and events, both observed and posited.
> A scientific theory is a structure suggested by these laws and is devised to explain
> them in a scientifically rational manner.

The problem with this formulation from an Economics perspective is that – as
argued in earlier chapters – there are no empirical laws and therefore no theories of this type. But it is possible to rewrite the statement above to capture
the spirit of the definition in the context of economics. This would lead to the
following interpretation of theory:

> Scientific theory, systematic ideational structure of broad scope, conceived by the
> human imagination. A scientific theory is a structure devised to help explain obser-
> vations and relations in a scientifically rational manner.

It also written:

> Thus, it is evident that theories are imaginative constructions of the human mind—
> the results of philosophical and aesthetic judgments as well as of observation—for
> they are only suggested by observational information.

This could be correct even if there are no laws in a certain scientific field.

In Wikipedia it is also said that "In everyday speech, the word 'theory' is
used as a 'best guess'".

6.3   THE USE OF THEORY (AND HYPOTHESIS) IN THE AER ARTICLES

The strategy in this study of the AER-articles is to first to present a quantitative picture of the use of theory/theoretical and then to identify different interpretations by looking closer at the contexts in which the words theory/theoretical were used in the articles. As theory can also be used in the same sense as a hypothesis, the study here also included that word.

6.3.1   How often theory and hypothesis are used

In the first step, I counted the number of times theory and theoretical were used in each article. The search were made using "theor" and "hypoth" and all occurrences were inspected to see that they were relevant for this study. Reference lists and similar parts of the articles were excluded. Table 6.1 show median, minimum and maximum numbers of occurrences for the three different types of articles identified in earlier chapters (model based, empirical, both model based and empirical) in 1990 and 2020.

Table 6.1   *The use of theory and hypothesis in different types of articles: median values and min–max in parentheses*

Type 1 articles	1990	2020
Theory	3 (0–16)	4 (0–49)
Hypothesis	0 (0–5)	0 (0–9)
Type 2 articles		
Theory	5 (0–14)	4 (0–61)
Hypothesis	11 (0–70)	1 (0–12)
Type 3 articles		
Theory	5 (0–24)	3 (0–40)
Hypothesis	4 (1–23)	3 (0–24)

A first general observation is that words such as *theory* and *theoretical* are used rather sparsely in the majority of the articles. The median value is 3–5 times in an article. As will be clear in the next chapter, the word *model* is used much more often.

There are no clear differences between the different types of articles. The Type 1 articles – where a mathematical model is constructed and analysed – are often called theoretical studies and it might therefore be somewhat surprising that the word theory is not used more often in that type of article. On the other hand, the empirical studies (Type 2 articles) can be expected to test a theory of some kind, so maybe the result that the word theory is used a little more often in the empirical studies is not so surprising after all.

There are no clear differences between 1990 and 2020. The median for the number of occurrences of theory increased somewhat for Type 1 articles, while it decreased somewhat for Type 2 and Type 3.

The picture is very different for the word *hypothesis*. If we first look at the articles from 1990, there are very large differences between the groups. In the majority of Type 1 articles, hypothesis is not mentioned at all, while the median number of times in Type 2 articles was 11. This result is perhaps what should be expected if the articles of Type 1 are seen as developing a theory and/or showing in what situations a certain relation holds, and if an empirical study is one where the researcher tests a certain hypothesis.

For Type 1 and Type 3 articles there are no clear changes over time, but there is a dramatic reduction in the use of the word *hypothesis* in the pure empirical studies. In order to understand what has happened, I re-read the abstract and introductory sections of a random selection of ten Type 2 articles from 2020 to see how they formulated what they were doing. The result is presented in Box 6.1.

BOX 6.1   INSTEAD OF THEORY AND HYPOTHESIS

One of the ten selected articles explicitly said that they were testing a hypothesis and one other referred to a theoretical framework. The role of this theoretical framework was to suggest possible explanations.

The most common formulation in the selected articles from 2020 was to say that – given a certain problem – they wanted to *estimate* something, typically to find out the effect of something or measure the strength of a certain relation. In some cases, the authors only said that they wanted to *study*, *measure* and/or *examine* something.

When the authors in the introduction summarized their results, the most common formulation was that the article/study contributes to various *literatures*. In these literatures there might be what could be called theories and/or hypotheses, but these words are not used by the authors.

There is a small number of articles that neither use the word theory/theoretical nor the word hypothesis anywhere in the articles and I thought that it should be of interest to try to understand how a researcher can present high class research in a world-leading journal without mentioning the words theory or hypothesis. If it is assumed that these articles are trying to accomplish the same thing as other articles of the same type, then the meaning of theory might be better understood if these alternative formulations are studied. Only articles from 2020 are included as these are the most relevant for the current situation in Economics. I have looked closer at how the purpose is described and how the researcher has described what they have done.

BOX 6.2   ARTICLES THAT DO NOT MENTION THEORY AND HYPOTHESIS ANYWHERE

In the three *Type 1* articles that do not mention theory or hypothesis the purpose is described as to *develop a model* or *present an analysis* that can explain, to *address* a certain questions and/or *study the effects* of a certain factor.

In the two other articles (one Type 2 and one Type 3) the purpose is described in terms of *identify* and *quantify* a certain relation, *do empirical tests* and/or *identify the impacts* of something or evaluate certain mechanisms.

In the next chapter I will look closer at the relation between theory and model in the articles, and in the concluding comments return to the question of the "theory-free" empirical studies.

6.3.2   Different Uses of Theory in the Articles

The words *theory* and/or *theoretical* are used in a large number of contexts in the studied articles. The following uses were identified after a close reading of the relevant parts of the articles.

Theory as something very general. Examples of the broadest use are references to economic theory (or the somewhat narrower: standard economic theory), sociological theory or statistical theory. On a somewhat lower level but still very general are references to game theory, theories of oligopoly, mechanism design theory, or theories of bargaining. It can also be references to a more specific school within economic theory, for example Keynesian theory, political business cycle theory or real business cycle theory. In the latter cases, the theory can be seen as something that included rather general empirical hypotheses about how the economy works.

Theories as frameworks. In the same way as in the Nobel Prize material there are in some articles references to or headlines referring to the (author's) theoretical framework. What this might mean is discussed in Section 6.5.

Theories as more specific hypotheses. Authors might write that they have a theory about what can explain a certain observation – and the theory then typically points out a certain factor or mechanism that can cause the fact to be explained.

In a few cases there is *a contrast between theory and practice.* It is for example claimed that something can work in theory, but for some reason it would not work in practice.

Another way to look at theory in the studied articles is to look at what is said about *what theory does.* Examples of formulation are that theory *suggests*, *explains*, *predicts*, can *rationalize,* or give a *rationale* for something and/or can help us *understand.*

In a few articles, theory is not referring to something that a scientist develops but *something that people have*: actors in a market are assumed to have a certain theory that determines their action in a specific situation.

The word *theoretical* also occurs in a large number of combinations, for example theoretical understanding, theoretical intuition, theoretical model, theoretical possibility, theoretical presumption, theoretical conclusion, rigorous theoretical structure, theoretical support, theoretical work, theoretical benchmark, theoretical insights and theoretical framework. Here is an attempt to interpret and systematize these different formulations.

Theoretical work can mean building a mathematical model but can also include a more general discussion about some phenomena, as in the articles by Williamson discussed earlier. A *theoretical conclusion* would simply be a conclusion from any of these types of theoretical works. These (simplified) theoretical works can also function as a *benchmark* for further studies. *Theoretical understanding* is what you reach after studying a theoretical work. A study of the theoretical work might also lead to a *theoretical intuition* or a *theoretical presumption* about what can be expected to happen in a certain empirical situation. This intuition/presumption can also be something that motivates the development of a specific theoretical or empirical work.

6.4   THE RELATION BETWEEN THEORY AND EMPIRICAL STUDIES IN THE AER ARTICLES

A simple view of science is that, first, a theory is formulated, and then empirical studies are carried out to test the theory. A theoretical article – Type 1 above – would then end by saying that the next step is an empirical test. An empirical article – Type 2 above – would start by saying that there is a certain untested theory and that the aim of the study is to test a certain theory. The question is now whether this is the typical formulations in the articles studied.

Looking first at Type 1 articles there are in some cases, at the end, a discussion about testable implications and empirical studies that could be made to investigate if (typically) the analysed mechanism in the model is important in the real-world market. Explicit comments of this type can however only be found in 11 of the 44 articles from 1990 (25 per cent). This kind of formulation is even rarer in 2020 where it can be found only in two of the 16 articles (12.5 per cent). As this is a very small sample, the change is not statistically significant at the 5 per cent level.

In the Type 2 articles it was expected that theories should be mentioned as something that motivates the empirical study. In some cases, a specific theory/ model was mentioned and in other cases more general references to theories was made. It could, however, also be the case that the study was motivated only by what is seen as an interesting economic question, for example with references to public debates or to disagreements between earlier empirical studies. In these cases there would be no mentioning of any specific theory or model.

In Table 6.2 it can be seen that, in the 1990 articles, around 50 per cent of the empirical articles refer to a theory of some kind in the introduction, but in 2020 this share had fallen to below 20 per cent. The change is statistically significant at the 5 per cent level. The criteria to call something theory-related were set low and it was not necessary to explicitly say that the aim was to test a certain theory – it was enough that a theory or model produced by earlier researchers was mentioned as part of the background of the study.

Table 6.2   *References to (testing of) theory in the aim of empirical articles*

	1990 number	2020 number	1990 percent	2020 percent
Theory mentioned	9	6	53	16
No theory mentioned	8	32	47	84
Total	17	38		

The conclusion from the results is that there is a rather weak link between theoretical and empirical studies in these articles, and as it is a highly ranked journal it would be surprising if the result does not reflect the situation in Economics more generally. It can, however, be observed that even when there were no references to theories in the introductory text there is, especially in the 2020 articles, a section where implications for different strands of literature are discussed. This discussion sometimes includes comments on implications for certain theories.

One possible explanation for the rather weak link between theoretical and empirical articles is that the two different activities *are two independent ways of making a point*. If a researcher wants to argue that there is a certain relation and/or that a certain mechanism is causing a certain phenomenon and/or that a policy will have a certain effect, this could be done in two ways: either show that the relation holds in a credible mathematical model or show that the relation holds in a certain empirical material. If these activities play the same role in making a certain link between two phenomena more credible, then there would be no direct link between them. Instead of one type of study (the theoretical) preceding the other (the empirical), these two types of studies could be carried out parallel to each other, and the only relation between them is that both concern the same relation, both try to strengthen a certain claim.

One could also speculate that a widening gap between theoretical/mathematical and empirical/statistical studies may be caused by increased specialization and compartmentalization. Both the mathematical methods and the statistical methods used seem to be more complex in the 2020 articles. It might then be logical for a researcher to specialize in one activity and primarily write for other researchers that work with the same type of studies. The important thing is then to relate to the same type of studies as one wants to improve on the earlier studies of this type. It would then also be logical to end with saying that further studies of the same type are needed in order to improve our knowledge.

6.5   THEORETICAL FRAMEWORKS: WHAT THEY ARE AND WHAT THEY ARE USED FOR

Both in the Nobel Prize motivations and in the AER-articles, concepts such as theoretical framework are used. The prizes were, for example, given to researchers who had developed a theoretical framework and the researchers in the AER-articles said that they were using a certain framework. An example of the first type of formulation can be found in the prize to Hart and Holmstrom (2016) where the following is written in the motivations for awarding the Nobel Prize:

> Contract theory does not necessarily provide definitive or unique answers to these questions, as the best contract will typically depend on the specific situation and context. However, the power of the theory is that it enables us to think clearly about the issues involved.

A first observation when looking at the AER-articles is that frameworks can be on *different levels*. Microeconomic theory or game theory can be seen as theoretical frameworks on a very general level, while contract theory can be seen as a framework on a somewhat less general level. In the AER articles, framework is sometimes used on a much more specific level and is then used for structuring a very specific research question.

Let us try to clarify what a theoretical framework is and what it does.[1] One way to approach this question for the most general types of frameworks is to think about what a student learns when they take courses in, for example, microeconomic theory on basic and intermediate levels. My hypothesis is that the typical student learns the following when they learn a general theoretical framework.

- They learn a number of *new concepts*, for example opportunity cost, utility maximizing, budget constraint, demand curve, price elasticity of demand, income effect and substitution effect, Pareto-efficiency, externality, public good, asymmetric information, moral hazard, random walk, and comparative advantage.
- They learn a number of *logical implications*, for example that utility maximizing consumer will – given certain assumptions – choose a basket of goods where the marginal utility of each good equals their price (or that the marginal rate of substitution will equal the price ratio), that a competitive market given certain assumptions leads to an efficient use of resources, that entry and exit leads to zero (economic) profit in the long run.
- They learn a number of *possible explanations*, for example why a demand or supply curve shifts and leads to changes in prices. The demand for a good might fall as incomes go up and the good is inferior, and a price increase might in certain situation lead to increased sales, for example if it is a Giffen good.
- They learn a number of *possible effects*, for example how a tax change for a specific good can affect price and production, the effects of price floors and price ceilings.
- They learn a number of *policy options*, for example how negative externalities or moral hazard can be counteracted.
- They learn a number of *techniques* by which one can analyse certain issues. In some basic textbooks there is mostly diagrammatic tools (such as supply and demand curves), but at least in more advanced courses they learn a number of mathematical tools and examples of how to use them. They learn a strategy by which to approach a question and a number of basic models that they can start from when trying to explain a certain observation.

---

[1] Theoretical frameworks are discussed in a similar way to below in Lind (1992) and then based on how frameworks were used in the articles studied there.

When looking at a theoretical framework on a less general level one should expect to find some *general empirical hypotheses* as part of the framework. In a Keynesian framework, assuming that prices are sticky can be such a central empirical assumption. In a real business cycle framework, random productivity shocks would be such an assumption.

My experience is furthermore that the claims that a microeconomic teacher makes about the theory can vary considerably. What one teacher, or researcher for that matter, sees as a rather good approximation can by another teacher be presented as something rather unrealistic, but still a good starting point for a more realistic analysis of certain phenomenon. My conclusion from this is that one cannot see, for example, microeconomic theory as something very specific: people may agree that microeconomics is important to teach and learn – but they may not agree why it is important. Each has their own interpretation of what the general theory really is: for some, it is just a starting point and for others a rather good approximation.

6.6   CONCLUDING COMMENTS

The philosopher of science, Ian Hacking, once wrote "we must never fall prey to the fallacy of talking about theory without making distinctions" (Hacking, 1983, p 183). In this chapter it was clear that, in Economics, *theory* can be used with rather different meanings, from a general framework that helps one structure a problem and suggest a research strategy, to a very specific hypothesis about what is the cause of something.

I think there are two especially important observation in this chapter. The first observation is that, in the AER articles, the words *theory* and *theoretical* does not play a very large role. The word *model*, which is discussed in the next chapter, is used much more often. Economists talk about building and investigating models rather than developing theory. They talk about estimating and measuring relations rather than testing a theory or hypothesis.

The second observation is the rather weak link between the different activities: those who build mathematical models seldom refers to empirical studies and those that do empirical studies seldom refer to theories (or models).

7. On models in Economics

7.1   INTRODUCTION

The word "model" (models, modelling) was used on average 40 times in the AER-articles from 1990 and 2020 (see Section 7.3 below). There have also been claims that Economics is a model-based science (Rodrick 2015), so there is no need to spend time arguing that it is important to look closer at the concept of a model and the use of different types of models in Economics.

As in the previous chapter, the starting point is discussions in some dictionaries about models and modelling in science in general in (Section 7.2). In Section 7.3, the uses of models in the AER-articles are described. Section 7.4 describes some views about models from the philosophical literature, and Section 7.5 discusses how results that something happens in a model can be evidence in relation to statements about a real economy. An informal Bayesian framework is introduced for this, and such a framework was used in the case study that is presented in Section 7.6. The idea that Economics is a model-based science is commented upon in Section 7.7 especially in light of the results from the studies of the AER-articles. Final comments can be found in Section 7.8.

7.2   MODELS ACCORDING TO SOME DICTIONARIES

A scientific model is typically described as something that is built to represent something. In *Brittanica* online it is written:

> Scientific modelling, the generation of a physical, conceptual, or mathematical representation of a real phenomenon that is difficult to observe directly. Scientific models are used to explain and predict the behaviour of real objects or systems and are used in a variety of scientific disciplines, ranging from physics and chemistry to ecology and the Earth sciences. Although modelling is a central component of modern science, scientific models at best are approximations of the objects and systems that they represent—they are not exact replicas. Thus, scientists constantly are working to improve and refine models.

In other definitions of model (see below) it is, however, not said that the model must represent a real phenomenon that is difficult to observe, or even that it must represent a real phenomenon at all. Concerning the purpose of modelling, the following is written:

> The purpose of scientific modelling varies. Some models, such as the three-dimensional double-helix model of DNA, are used primarily to visualize an object or system, often being created from experimental data. Other models are intended to describe an abstract or hypothetical behaviour or phenomenon. For example, predictive models, such as those employed in weather forecasting or in projecting health outcomes of disease epidemics, generally are based on knowledge and data of phenomena from the past and rely on mathematical analyses of this information to forecast future, hypothetical occurrences of similar phenomena.

In the *Modern Stanford dictionary of philosophy* there is a long entry on Models in science and the following seems to be the most interesting parts from the perspective of (primarily theoretical) models in Economics. The focus is then on mathematical models, such as those found in what I call Type 1 articles. In the Dictionary, they write "A time-honored position has it that a model is a stylized description of a target system".

A number of different "types" of models are then described, for example:

- *Idealized models* defined as "models that involve a deliberate simplification or distortion of something complicated with the objective of making it more tractable or understandable". It is also argued that idealization is closely related to approximation.
- *Toy models* "are extremely simplified and strongly distorted renderings of their targets, and often only represent a small number of causal or explanatory factors". These models have also been characterized as "caricatures".
- *Minimal models* "are closely related to toy models in that they are also highly simplified. They are so simplified that some argue that they are non-representational: they lack any similarity, isomorphism, or resemblance relation to the world. It has been argued that many economic models are of this kind".
- *Exploratory models* "are models which are not proposed in the first place to learn something about a specific target system or a particular experimentally established phenomenon. Exploratory models function as the starting point of further explorations in which the model is modified and refined."

If the starting point is a typical "theoretical" model in Economics – where a number of assumptions are made and a number of relations are proven – these different "types" of models can also be described in terms of *different claims about what the presented (mathematical) model is, and different claims about what the analysis of the model accomplish.* This will be discussed more in detail later in this chapter.

7.3   THE USE OF THE TERM MODEL IN THE AER ARTICLES

7.3.1   A Quantitative Analysis

The word "model" is used very frequently in the AER articles both in 1990 and 2020, much more frequently than "theory" and "hypothesis". There is no clear difference between the years, except that the word is used more often in the Type 1 articles in 2020. As can be seen in Table 7.1, there is a systematic difference between the three types of articles. The median value of the number of times model or modelling was mentioned in 2020 was 40 for Type 1 articles (mathematical models only), eight for Type 2 articles (empirical studies only) and 63 for Type 3 articles that both contain an analysis of a mathematical model and an empirical estimation.

Table 7.1   The use of model/modelling in different types of articles: median values with min-max in parentheses

	1990	2020
Type 1 articles		
Model/modelling	24 (2–158)	40 (6–279)
Type 2 articles		
Model/modelling	11 (0–283)	8 (0–140)
Type 3 articles		
Model/modelling	67 (3–224)	63 (10–262)

There is no article of Type 1 or of Type 3 where the word "model" or "modelling" does not occur. The word occurs more than 250 times in those articles where the word is used most frequently.

There are no explicit discussions about what is meant by a model in the AER-articles, but from the formulation and the context several types can be identified, as described in the next section.

7.3.2   The Meaning of the Term Model/Modelling

7.3.2.1   Use of model in articles of Type 1
The articles in this category all contain the presentation and analysis of a mathematical model. Assumptions are made and relations are proven – often

described as theorems. It is therefore not surprising that the word "model" or "modelling" occurs many times in these articles, and that the term typically refers to this kind of mathematical model. In many articles a "baseline model" is presented and then variations are analysed.

The term model also occurs in combinations that describe what type of model it is; for example, that it is a *dynamic* model, *Keynesian* model, *game-theoretic* model, *Stackelberg* model, *standard classroom* model, *simple* model, *choice-theoretic* model, *overlapping generation* model, *cash-in-advance* model, *life-cycle* model, *multi-agent contracting* model, *Bayesian* model or *canonical* model.

These uses can be divided into some sub-groups. Some refer to the *complexity* of the model (for example simple model, standard classroom model), some refer to the *general structure* of the model (for example dynamic model, game-theoretic model), some refer to the *more detailed structure* of the model (for example overlapping generation model, cash-in advance model) and in some cases the addition concerns *more specific assumptions made in the model* (e.g. Keynesian model, Stackelberg model).

There is also the combination "*formal* model" and if that is interpreted as a mathematical model where relations are proven, then all the models in the articles in this group are formal models. The description "*consistent theoretical* model" is also used in a few places and it should refer to the same thing.

In a few cases, the word model does not refer to a mathematical model but to a certain real-world structure. In an article it is, for example, said that manufacturing is undergoing a revolution and that the *mass production model* is increasingly being replaced. As mentioned in the theory section, a model can also refer to assumptions that an actor has: the individual or the firm makes certain assumptions about a certain situation and this model/theory then determines the actions of that individual/firm.

7.3.2.2 The relation between a theory and a model in Type 1 articles

There are several different formulations in this context. The most common is formulations such as "game-theoretic model" and this should be interpreted as that the model has a certain structure and is based on assumptions from the theory referred to. A formulation such as a "theoretical model that formalizes auction theory" points in the same direction.

There are also cases where the distinction between theory and model seems to be non-existent. In one article, the title refers to a model of x while the author in the introduction writes about a theory of x. Another example is that "Keynesian model" and "Keynesian theory" are used interchangeably in some articles. One author writes about "standard two-by-two Heckscher-Ohlin trade theory", but only a few pages later the author writes about the "standard two-by-two Heckscher-Ohlin model". Another example is the following formulation: "This paper offers an equilibrium theory which preserves some basic insights from earlier models".

A general discussion about the relation between models and theories can be found in the Stanford Dictionary quoted above. They write that some philosophers of science have argued that models primarily serve a pedagogic purpose, and that all relevant information is contained in the theory. A more interesting view from the perspective of Economics is that *a theory simply is a family of models*, a view that I will return to in Section 7.7. In the dictionary it is also argued that models can be independent from theories and an example is presented where the model "was constructed using only relatively common-sensical assumptions about [...] and [...] and the mathematics of differential equations". Another view described is that a model is more preliminary and may change into a theory if it gets more empirical support.

7.3.2.3 The use of model in the empirical articles (Type 2)

In these articles it is common to use the term model when the equations to be estimated are presented; for example, in combinations such as *econometric* model or *statistical* model.

These models can then be classified in a number of ways on order to describe the kind of approach used, for example a *difference in difference* model, a *probit* model, a *DSGE*-model or a *VAR*-model.

In the rest of this chapter the focus will be on the mathematical models used in Type 1 articles.

7.3.3   Concluding Comments on the AER-articles

In the AER articles, the authors do not discuss the meaning and role of models in general, but focus only on why the specific model in their articles adds something in relation to the earlier studies of the same type in their specific research field. This is, of course, what we should expect in "normal science".

Mathematical model building is seen as an established method and not in need of explanation. There is only a need to explain why the current model leads to more interesting results than earlier models. As described in earlier chapters, these arguments typically point out that the new model is more realistic than earlier models in some relevant dimension and/or that the new assumptions fit a situation that earlier models did not cover. It was also rather common to argue that the new model was based on a mathematical technique that is easier to work with and/or more flexible.

As discussed in the previous chapter, theory can be used in a number of different ways and, based on distinctions made there, one could say the following about possible relations between theory and mathematical models built in

Type 1 articles. Notice, however, that clear formulations of these types cannot be found in the articles studied.

A *theoretical framework* may be the starting point for the construction of the specific model, for example when a game-theoretic model is built.

A *general theory* about what are important factors or realistic assumptions can determine some assumptions in the model, for example when it is said that it is a Keynesian model or a real-business-cycle model.

A *specific theory* about what determines an observed phenomena can be formalized in the model: a new feature is added to the model and then it is shown that a model including this feature can explain the observed phenomenon.

7.4   INTERPRETATIONS OF "THEORETICAL MODELS" IN ECONOMICS: COMMENTS ON SOME VIEWS IN THE METHODOLOGICAL LITERATURE

The model in Type 1 articles is a mathematical structure where an imagined economy is described through a set of assumptions. The researcher then uses various mathematical tools and mathematical theorems to prove that certain relations hold in the model economy. There is a large methodological literature about such models, but I will focus on a few works that often are quoted and also are rather recent. The first work is "Credible worlds: the status of theoretical models in economics" (Sugden 2000).

7.4.1   Main Arguments in Sugden (2000)

Two very simplified and very famous models are discussed in this article: Schelling's model of segregation on the housing market and Akerlof's lemon model of the used car market. Sugden writes:

> I believe that each of these models tells us something important and true about the real world. My object is to discover just what these models do tell us about the world, and how they do it. (p. 2)

Sugden's starting point is that models (primarily) are built to help us understand how the real economy works – which seems to be a reasonable starting point given the results in Chapters 2, 3 and 4 above. The question is then how a simplified and in certain respects unrealistic model can help us understand how the real world works. He writes:

> Each uses a formal model in support of the claim of causation. (p. 8)

He furthermore formulates the task as follows:

> Somehow a transition has to be made from a particular hypothesis, which has been shown to be true in the model world, to a general hypothesis, which we can expect to be true in the real world. (p. 19)

I do not think that this is a good way of formulating the problem. The view that will be argued for below is instead that the starting point for the researcher is a (rather) general hypothesis about the real world. The result in the model can then be seen as *evidence* for this claim about the real world – evidence that can be stronger or weaker depending on a number of circumstances that I will return to below. But let us continue with Sugden's view.

Sugden (2000, p. 19) argues that there must be some kind of inductive leap and that this could be motivated in several ways, for example that the results in the model are robust. Sugden's central thesis is however that:

> So what might increase our confidence in such inferences? I want to suggest that we can have more confidence in them, the greater the extent to which we can understand the relevant model as a description of how the world *could be*. (p. 24, emphasis in original)
>
> The suggestion of this paper is that the gap between model world and real world can be filled by inductive inference. ... They [the models] describe credible counterfactual worlds. This credibility gives us some warrant for making inductive inferences from model to real world. (p. 28)

If one is thinking in Bayesian terms the suggestion would instead be: the result that a certain relation holds in the model can be seen as new information that makes it rational to change the probability of one or more empirical statements. One factor that affects how much it is rational to change the probability is how robust the result is (see further discussions in Sections 7.5 and 7.6).

7.4.2   Main thesis in Mäki (2009)

In the methodological literature, Uskali Mäki has, in several articles, discussed this kind of economic model. His general view is similar to the ideas in Sugden's article and this is clear from the title of one of his articles "MISSing the world. Models as isolations and credible surrogate systems" (Mäki 2009).[1] Models are, according to this view, built and analysed in order to help us understand how the world works. He calls them "isolation models".

---

[1]   Mäki's work is analysed from a number of different perspective in the book *Economics for Real: Uskali Mäki and the place of truth in economics* (Lehtinen et al. 2016).

Mäki underlines the pragmatic context in which a model is used, and presents the following general formulation for describing the different parts of this context and the claims made about a specific model (p. 32):

> Agent A
> uses object M as
> a representative of some target system R
> for purpose P,
> addressing audience E,
> prompting genuine issues of resemblance to arise
> and applies commentary C to identify and align these components.

The purpose P of the modelling can be any of the purposes presented initially in this chapter – from creating a pedagogical device to creating something that is claimed to be an approximation. The focus in the discussion here is, however, on cases where the purpose is to increase our knowledge about the real economy. The idea in Mäki's article is that even if there are a number of simplifications in the model the mechanism in the model *resembles* or *corresponds* to (p. 32) the target system in suitable respects and to sufficient degrees. These resemblances and correspondences are typically clarified in what Mäki calls the "commentary" that the author includes in the article. Mäki writes that for this commentary "More specific information is needed, based on empirical inquiries into specific cases".

I am not sure that the words "resembles" or "corresponds to" add much content, but I think that it is a very important point that there is a "commentary" in the typical model-based article. In the next section I look closer at a number of the commentaries in the AER-articles.

In an anthology about Mäki's methodological works (Lehtinen et al., 2016), Lehtinen writes the following in the introduction:

> Mäki's primary motivation for developing an account of models and modelling is to show that there are ways in which models can be taken to be true even though they contain various false assumptions and even when their predictions are false. (Lehtinen, 2016, p. 27)

From my Bayesian perspective, one can – as mentioned above – see the result about relations in a model as evidence for statements about the real world, but it seems very strange to say that a model "could be taken as true" if there is a number of simplified and unrealistic assumptions. I am far from sure that Mäki would formulate himself in that way. I would rather say that the result that there is a certain relation in the model might be strong and convincing evidence for a statement about a real economy – but that all depends on the information given in "the commentary" to the mathematical model.

7.5   LOOKING AT "COMMENTARIES" IN TYPE 1 ARTICLES

In order to get an idea about what a commentary in a Type 1 article typically is, I looked closer at a random selection of five of the 16 articles from 2020 that all started with an empirical observation and then built a model to cast light on this real-world issue. In these articles, it is shown that in a model with certain assumptions, A leads to B through the mechanism M. There is a lot of simplifications in the model and the question is then how it is argued that the result in the model is relevant for understanding how the real-world works.

The authors' comments relate to several different issues. The author can present empirical examples of cases where A seems to have led to B. In some cases, there are references to things that are known from a number of studies ("a well-documented empirical fact") or that other studies present "suggestive evidence".

Concerning the specific assumptions in the model, the motivations focus on what is new in the model. Standard assumptions in a certain literature or in a specific type of model are not commented upon at all. Sometimes it is argued – with references to empirical studies or casual observations – that the new assumption is more realistic, or that there are certain situations where the new assumption is more realistic. Empirical studies "indicate" that the assumption is rather realistic. Some of these arguments are similar to the type of general knowledge that a court would not demand specific evidence for in a court case (see the next section). Sometimes models are not presented as alternatives to earlier models but as complementary by adding results from somewhat different assumptions. Sometimes they are presented as more general where the old models are special cases.

It is common with comments about the robustness of the results in relation to certain specific assumptions. One can find at least three different versions of such claims: (1) it has been shown in other articles that the result is robust to this specific assumption; (2) there are general reasons to believe that the result is robust (an intuition); or (3) the robustness will be investigated in future studies.

As underlined above, not all assumptions are commented on, and from a rhetorical perspective one could guess that the authors focus on the assumptions that they believe that other researchers might question.

7.6   AN ATTEMPT TO SYSTEMATIZE HOW RESULTS IN A MODEL CAN BE SEEN AS EVIDENCE

If we focus on the question of how we can learn about the real world through the type of mathematical models that are common in economics, I suggest that this should be analysed in the same way as a court evaluates the strength of a certain piece of evidence. There are of course different theories about how this should be done, but one of the common frameworks start from Bayes theorem. I have used a leading Swedish advanced textbook as a starting point: The book *Power of Evidence* by Dahlman (2018).

If we apply this framework to the mathematical models in economics, then – as said above –the proven result in the model should be seen as *new information*. There is an underlying hypothesis about a relation in the real economy and in a Bayesian framework the researcher assigns this hypothesis a prior probability. The question then becomes how much it is rational to change this prior probability given the new information that a certain relation holds in a specific model.

One important aspect of the Bayesian framework is that evidence can be stronger or weaker, but the evidence is seldom conclusive and seldom completely worthless. The question is whether the result in the mathematical model should be seen as *strong* evidence or only rather *weak* evidence for the hypothesis that there is a certain relation in the real world.

If I try to translate the arguments in Dahlmans's book to the current situation the result would be the following:

1. There are certain statements where explicit evidence is not needed. These statements are seen as general knowledge, for example that a statement by a witness is more reliable if the lighting is good. In the same way economists "know" a lot of things about people, companies and the economy from experience or reading certain types of material. It can therefore be seen as obvious that a certain assumption is (rather) realistic. Williamson's statement that there is a risk for opportunistic behaviour in organisations might belong to this category.
2. The result from a model is stronger evidence if it can be argued that at least some central assumptions in the model is rather realistic given what has been found in empirical studies of different types.
3. The result from a rather unrealistic model is stronger evidence if there are reasons to believe that the unrealistic assumptions do not matter for the result. Such assumptions are typically called harmless assumptions. The argument here can be that the assumption has been shown to be harmless in other cases or simply that it is obvious for any well-informed person that it is highly unlikely that a change in this specific assumption would

change the result in the model. The question of harmlessness is related to the next point.

4.   The result from a model is stronger evidence if the results are rather robust. The assumptions can then be changed in a number of ways, but the result still holds. This is, as mentioned above, especially important if the assumption is not obviously harmless.

5.   The result from the model is stronger evidence if there are no competing models that can also explain B. That A leads to B in a model would not be strong evidence for A being the cause of B if there are other (credible) models where B instead is caused by C.

McCloskey (1994) formulated a theorem that said that for every model where A leads to B there is another model infinitely close to the first model where A does not lead to B. If that theorem were true, then the evidential value of the new information that A leads to B in the model would be very low. There is, however, no reason to believe that McCloskey's theorem is true, but it points to the importance of checking the robustness of the result and possible alternative mechanisms before one gives the new information high evidential value. The issue is also discussed in McCloskey (2022, p 35).

Both Sugden and Mäki discuss Schelling's model(s) of residential segregation. A possible Bayesian interpretation of the hypothesis and evidence in this case is the following. Suppose initially that the dominating view is that residential segregation is caused by strong preferences against living close to people from the other group. Schelling then formulates a competing hypothesis: that a certain mechanism can led to large-scale segregation even if people do not mind having some neighbours from the other group as long as some other neighbours are from their own group.

To make this claim credible Schelling presents a combination of everyday examples and a mathematical model where complete segregation results even though people do not mind having one of two neighbours from the other group. The model is very simplified and unrealistic in a number of respects. The model can still lead to a large increase in the probability of the hypothesis if (a) the behavioural assumptions seem reasonable based on many people's everyday observations, (b) the conclusion is or can be expected to be robust to changes in a number of the specific assumptions made. One can imagine that, over the years, other economists have tried to construct competing models with the same behavioural assumptions but other institutional settings. If it turns out to be very difficult to create such a model that gives another result, then the probability of the hypothesis is increased more if the hypothesis is true in the "only" credible model that researchers have been able to construct.

Dahlman especially points out that the probability of a hypothesis depends on the availability of other hypotheses. In the literature on segregation such hypotheses can be found; for example, that segregation is related to discrimination and gate-keeping. If Schelling's statement however only is that actual large-scale segregation *can* arise even though people are rather tolerant, the truth of his proposition will not depend on the availability of other hypotheses like the ones just mentioned.

The kind of information found in commentaries presented in Section 7.5 is just what we should expect given this Bayesian framework. In these commentaries the authors try to argue that the result is robust to specific assumptions made and they try to argue that some assumptions are reasonable given the existing empirical evidence. Many also start with pointing out problems in existing hypotheses and that competing hypotheses are not as credible as their own. The problems in the earlier models were typically described as that crucial assumptions were not credible and/or that the result was not robust to changes in some important assumptions.

One important implication of the last point is that the evidential value of a model cannot be evaluated just by looking at the model and how good approximations the assumptions are: by looking at how "true" the model is. The evidential value also depends on the availability of competing hypotheses. It is a very large difference between a situation where there is only one model with a credible mechanism and a situation where there are competing models that both contain credible mechanisms. In the latter case what is needed is probably more empirical information the can increase the credibility of one of the models and reduce the credibility of the other.

7.7   DOES A MODEL ADD TO KNOWLEDGE ABOUT THE REAL ECONOMY? A CASE STUDY

The hypothesis in theoretical Economics is that knowing what happens in a model helps us understand what happens in the real world. If this hypothesis is true or not can only be judged on a case-by-case basis. Let us assume that at a certain point in time there exists a certain amount of empirical knowledge in a field. A number of statements in this area can be ascribed a specific probability. If a mathematical model is now built where certain relations are proved one could say that this result increases our knowledge of how the world works *if the results from the model change the probability of empirical statements in the field.* In the example above, Shelling's model increased the probability of the hypothesis that extreme segregation can exist even if people prefer to live in a more mixed neighbourhood.

In order the evaluate if a model, or set of models, adds to our knowledge in this sense one has to be an expert in the field. One has to know the state of knowledge in the field and be able to relate the results from the models to that existing knowledge. When I was working with an article about rent regulation and new construction (Lind 2003) it struck me that I could do such an evaluation of (new) mathematical models about rent regulation – as I was one of the leading experts in that field with several often-quoted articles in international housing journals.

This led to the article "The story and the model done: An evaluation of mathematical models of rent regulation" (Lind 2007). As the title suggests, the evaluation does not concern the articles as such. The articles may contain new, interesting ideas – a new "story" – but the question that my study was concerned with was only *what the (results) from the mathematical models added.* My study uses an informal Bayesian framework as sketched in Section 7.6 where the result from the mathematical analysis is seen as new information and the question is then how this new information changes the probability of relevant empirical propositions.

The eight articles studied are of Type 1 according to the classification used in this book. A list of the articles can be found in the Appendix and are named A1 to A8. The contributions of the articles (see Table 2 in Lind 2007) are also described as being of the same type as was described in the earlier chapters in this book. The new thing is either that a different type of rent regulation is studied or that the effects are analysed in a different setting than in earlier studies. Conclusions are – as in the AER-articles – often formulated as the analysis shows that something *can* explain or *can* lead to something.

In order to use a Bayesian framework, certain propositions must be the starting point – and the evaluation leaves open the questions of whether the models add to knowledge in relation to other propositions. In Lind (2007) it is first noted that the results in the articles add to knowledge in relation to some very simple general hypotheses. Assume that the proposition in question is:

P1: Rent regulation will in all circumstances lead to lower housing construction.

If an article then shows that, in a specific model, rent regulation does not lead to lower construction then then researcher has shown that proposition P1 is false: the probability of the statement has been reduced to zero.

In my experience, this kind of general statement is seldom asserted in practical/political discussions about rent regulation. Statements in these debates typically concern the effect of a specific type of rent regulation in a certain country. This means that even though an article changes the probability of a statement such as P1, it does not necessarily change the probability of any "interesting" statement about rent regulation that is part of actual controversies about rent regulation.

A more interesting proposition (P2) and counter-proposition (P3) presented in the article are (somewhat simplified) is the following:

P2: In (many) actual rental markets (many) households have high moving costs. The landlord can therefore charge a rent higher than the market level when a contract expires. Rent regulations can therefore improve the welfare for tenants.

P3: A landlord who would charge a rent higher than the market rent for sitting tenants would get a bad reputation and therefore have to set lower initial rents. Therefore it would not be profitable for the landlord to charge more than the market rent when a contract is renewed.

Several of the analysed articles present a model that shows that in that model – where no reputation effects are included – P2 is true. But these results would not change the probabilities of statements P2 and P3. In order to do that, a reputation mechanism would have to be included in the model, but none of the studied articles did that.

More examples and more detailed arguments can be found in the article, but there is no reason to replicate them here as I just want to describe a possible way to evaluate a claim that knowledge of what happens in a model will increase our knowledge of the real economy.

The conclusion from the study was rather negative. The results from the analysis of the models did not change the probability of propositions that were judged to be central in public debates about rent regulation. As I will return to in the final section, maybe the models would have been more interesting if the authors had more "institutional knowledge" and had focused more on what was controversial propositions in public debates about rent regulation.

It should be remembered that my study only concerned a small number of studies in a very specific area in relation to a small number of propositions. The strategy used in my article could however be used for evaluating how much results from a mathematical model changed the probability of specific empirical hypotheses in other fields.

In my article there is also a short comment about asymmetric information and principal agent problems in advanced Economics. If an economist builds an advanced mathematical model and claims that the result shed light on and increases our understanding of a specific real world problem, how can even other economists evaluate if the claim is correct? As I see it, this is an important argument for putting more effort into writing a good "commentary" when a model is presented.

7.8 IS IT MODELS THAT MAKE ECONOMICS A SCIENCE?

One of the central claims in Rodrik (2015) is that "What makes economics a science is models" (p. 83). Later he also writes that "Theories are really just models" (p. 144) and makes the following comment about game theory, contract theory and growth theory: "In reality, each one of these is simply a particular collection of models" (p. 144).

As we saw at the beginning of this chapter, "model" can mean a number of different things and saying that models make Economics a science is then not a very clear statement. From the context in Rodrik's book, it is however rather clear that what he refers to are mathematical models such as those found in Type 1 articles.

Given the results in my empirical studies presented in this and earlier chapters, the claim that this kind of model makes Economics a science seems false. The study of the AER articles showed that a large share of the empirical studies made no reference to such models. The starting point was often just a question of general interest, an idea about a cause and an empirical design that should make it possible to reach knowledge about that issue. There have also been rather recent Nobel Prize winners – Williamson and Ostrom – who were not working with that kind of model.

It is easy to agree with Rodrik that in, for example, game theory there is a collection of such mathematical models that can be useful in a number of ways in a number of situations. If one looks at a standard medium level textbook in game theory, such as Tadelis (2013), it is filled with mathematical models, but game theory is there presented as a *theory* focusing on certain specific situations (interaction between a small number of actors) and the book introduces a large number of concepts and distinctions between different types of game situations. For me, it seems more correct to say that game theory *focuses on certain situations, introduces a number of concepts and ideas and that these concepts and ideas are illustrated, clarified and developed through the use of mathematical models*. The models are one part of the theory, but the theory cannot be reduced to a set of models.

A more common-sense view than Rodrik's would then be that what makes Economics a science is the aim to find out how economies work, a number of *ideas* about important causal factors in a number of situations and *methods* that can help us get knowledge of the world – and one of these methods is to build "theoretical" mathematical models.

If one asks what makes a certain study a study in Economics I think that Wittgenstein's concept of family resemblance is very useful. There is a network of similarities between studies that we see as Economics' studies

– concerning questions asked, basic ideas, methods used, etc. – but there is nothing that all these studies have in common. It can still be Economics even if a paper studies a question outside the traditional economic field if it uses economics concepts and methods. Becker was an example of this. And it is also Economics if a new method is used to study an old question – such as Smith's introduction of a laboratory experiment to study classic questions about how markets work. Thinking about Economics as consisting of studies characterized by family resemblance also creates openness and makes room for innovation. The researcher can introduce new ideas and methods but still be seen as part of Economics as there are resemblances with earlier studies in a number of respects.

Another idea in Rodrik's book is that economists start with the collection of models and then select the model that seems most suitable given the specific situation at hand. He also gives examples of such a process. More general discussion from a more philosophical perspective about how models can be selected can be found in, for example, Grüne-Yanoff and Marchionni (2018), Rodrik (2018) and Veit (2021).

If the idea of model selection is given a narrow interpretation, it does not get support from the study of the AER-articles. The articles do not start with a discussion about different possible models and with a selection process that leads to the chosen model. The researcher typically starts from one specific line in earlier research and a specific type of model, observes an anomaly and then creates a new model within this tradition aiming to solve the problem at hand by adjusting an earlier model in some respect. In some cases, the researcher explicitly starts from a certain research/modelling tradition – for example, earlier real business cycle models, earlier new Keynesian models or earlier efficient market models – and then proposes certain modifications in order to explain the observed anomaly without changing fundamental features of the earlier models in the tradition. When the researchers make these adjustments to solve the problem at hand, the researcher often uses general ideas in more modern economic theory and incorporates a specific version of that idea in the model. It can, for example, be that the researcher adds information problems, adjustments costs or various behavioural factors.

Instead of saying that Economics develops through adding more and more models, one could argue that economics develops through adding new ideas. These ideas are illustrated, made more credible or shown to be interesting by incorporating them in a specific mathematical model. The researcher, when working with a specific problem, picks the idea that seems to be fruitful for explaining the issue at hand and incorporates this idea in the kind of model that is typically used to study that specific question.

If this is correct, the main problem for the researcher is not to choose the right model to start from, but to find the new idea that has the potential to explain a certain anomaly. This will be illustrated in the case study of Krugman presented in the next chapter.

7.9 SUMMARY AND CONCLUDING COMMENTS ON MODELLING AND INSTITUTIONAL KNOWLEDGE

The main results in this chapter are the following:

- The word model/modelling is used very frequently in the studied AER-articles. The median number of times is around 40, but there are cases where the word is used more than 10 times per page.
- There are two main contexts where the word is used. The first is where the core of the article is the construction and analysis of relations in a mathematical model, and the second is an econometric/statistical model that is formulated and estimated in empirical articles. In this chapter/book the focus is on the first type of model.
- In earlier chapters we have seen that the aim of such a theoretical model-based study typically is to explain something and, for example, point to a possible cause of some anomaly that has been observed. The conclusion is often formulated as that the analysis suggests or indicates that a certain factor is the cause.
- In the philosophy of Economics literature, such mathematical models have been called "isolation models". The model focuses on one mechanism that can produce a certain result and leaves out other mechanisms. As will be clear in the next chapter, this is not true of all models of this type, as some models try to integrate different mechanisms. In earlier chapters, it was also seen that adding a feature to existing models was a common type of contribution and calling the new more complex model an isolation model may not be the best description.
- In the general philosophical literature about models it is pointed out that models in science can have many purposes. It can, for example, be claimed that the model is good for pedagogical purposes, that it is a good illustration of an idea/mechanism, that it is a starting point for constructing more realistic models or that the model is a good approximation of a certain real situation/process/market. This means that a model cannot be analysed in isolation. One has to look at the claims made about the model in a certain text. The claims made can change over time and vary between researchers even if the model is the same.
- The models in Type 1 articles that aim at increasing our knowledge of how a real economy works can be analysed with an informal Bayesian framework. The result that certain relations hold in a specific model-economy is then seen as new information, and the next question is then how much it is

rational to change the probability of certain empirical statements given this new information.

- As pointed out in the philosophy of economics literature, a model that is presented in an article is typically accompanied by a "commentary". Besides making the purpose and claims clearer, this commentary can discuss how good an approximation certain assumptions are, how robust the relations in the models are, and the commentary can include a comparison with competing hypotheses. The commentary is important for judging how much it is rational to change the probability of the empirical statements given the proven relations in the model.

A final comment concerning the evaluation of studies using a mathematical model (Type 1 articles) concerns a statement in Rodrik (2015). He writes that the model should focus on the *most relevant aspects* (p. 119) and that the models highlight the *dominant* causal mechanism (p. 85), but how does the researcher know what is the most relevant aspects or the dominant mechanism? Rodrik (2015) says that "the thinking that produced the model involved a large element of induction" (p. 659). There is, however, in the book no systematic discussion about what information this induction is based on. In a commentary there should be some kind of empirical information that substantiates a claim that a model includes the most relevant aspects and the dominant causal mechanisms. At least there should be a discussion about what information is needed and how it can be collected.

In the motivation of awarding the Nobel Prize to Jean Tirole, it is said that Tirole is a good example of an economist who was careful with designing his theoretical models to fit the institutional structure of a specific market. Nothing is, however, said about how the information about the institutional structure was collected.

There is a comment in the Nobel Prize texts about a question that Oliver Williamson had raised about when one should build theoretical models. In the SJE text about Williamson (Gibbons 2010) it is written.

> Williamson's contributions to TCE [Transaction Cost Economics] are a counter-example to Krugman's ... dictum "Like it or not, . . . the influence of ideas that have not been embalmed in models soon decays"....... [Williamson was] cautioning against "prematurely formal theory [that] purports to deal with real phenomena without doing the hard work of making serious contact with the issues" (p. 281)

The underlying issue is how much one needs to know about the institutional detail in order to build an interesting mathematical model. Williamson's idea seemed to be that constructing mathematical models should be done in a rather late stage of the research process if the aim is to help us understand how a specific market works. First, you need to make more qualitative studies about how the specific market works, for example by doing interviews with people working in the sector. It should then be important for doctoral students in Economics that are interested in building mathematical models to learn about how to collect the kind of information that is needed to evaluate whether a model is capturing "the most important aspects" and makes a "reasonable assumption" or not if it is an assumption that might be crucial. My guess is that most doctoral students in Economics learn very little about how information about such institutional knowledge should be collected. It is, however, interesting to see that several recent articles discuss how to use more qualitative information when building models (Donaldson 2022; Mahoney 2022; Todd & Wolpin 2023).

A final observation: In the early 1990s I moved from the Department of Economics at Stockholm University to the Department of Real Estate and Construction Management at KTH. One difference that struck me was the much closer contact between the KTH researchers and industry representatives in the broad sense. We had seminars with CEOs from companies and leading persons in the Tenant's union. We had reference groups with industry people in many projects. They pointed out unrealistic assumptions or aspects that we had not been aware of. Most Master's theses were based on interviews with people working in the sector. Research was continuously presented in business journals. The department also had a section working with real estate law, so we could easily get information about legal rules and their interpretation, including recent court cases. After working a number of years in this kind of department one had a large network of people that one could easily ask about how things "really work". Over the years, I was contacted a number of times by former colleagues from Stockholm University and other economists who wanted me to check whether they had misunderstood how something really worked in the housing market when they built various models. As they asked me about this, I concluded that they had no direct contact with people in companies or organizations that knew these things better than I did.

8. How to make an idea credible: a case study of Krugman's New Trade Theory

8.1 INTRODUCTION

One way to get a better understanding of Economics is to look closer at how a certain theory came to be generally accepted. I have chosen Krugman's trade theory because the story of the theory and its development is described in two of the documents that were published when Krugman was awarded the Nobel Prize. The first is the "Advanced information" published by the Swedish Academy of Sciences, and the second is Neary's article about the contribution of Krugman that was published at the same time in the *Scandinavian Journal of Economics*. Neary's article was called: "Putting the 'new' into New Trade Theory: Paul Krugman's Nobel memorial prize in economics" (Neary 2009). Krugman also received the Nobel Prize for his contribution to urban economics, but the focus in this book is only on his contribution to trade theory. To understand the process better I have also looked at some of the articles and books that are described as especially important in the "Advanced information" and in Neary's article.

The main idea in the new theory was that trade can be caused by economies of scale and heterogenous preferences, and that this type of trade can improve welfare in the same way as when trade is determined by the countries' comparative advantages.

8.2 THE BACKGROUND

The Nobel Prize documents underline two features of the theories that dominated before the new theory was presented. The central explanation for trade was then comparative advantages, and explanations of comparative advantages were in terms of different factor endowments. This theory implies that trade should be large between countries with different factor endowments and that exports and imports should consist of very different goods.

From a modelling perspective the earlier trade models were also dominated by models assuming perfect competition (Neary 2009, p. 217). Neary writes:

> However, a prerequisite for [the development of the new theory] was an analytic framework which would allow for both increasing returns to scale and differentiated products. (Neary 2009, p. 219)

This framework was Chamberlain's theory about monopolistic competition, but:

> What was needed was a tractable specification of preferences and costs which would make it possible to apply Chamberlin's insights at the global level, and the technical tools for doing just that were first assembled by Dixit and Stiglitz (1977). (Neary 2009, p. 220)

When trade flows were analysed empirically it was found that a lot of trade consisted of similar countries trading in similar goods. A typical example is that a country both imports and exports cars, targeting private households. This kind of trade was an anomaly from the perspective of the dominating trade theory.

When industrial goods dominate in both imports and exports, the assumption of homogeneous goods and perfect competition also seemed more and more unrealistic.

From both these perspectives the time was ripe for a new theory, and Neary (2009, p. 220) writes:

> What was needed was a master-chef to take these ingredients and use them to construct a new theory of trade.

8.3   KRUGMAN'S EARLY ARTICLES

8.3.1   Why a Mathematical Model

In three of his earlier articles (Krugman 1979, 1980, 1981), Krugman emphasizes that the idea that economies of scale can cause trade is not new. In Krugman (1979) he mentions Balasssa (1967) and Kravis (1971). In the motivation for awarding the Nobel Prize, Ohlin (1933) is also referred to. It is also noted that the theory fits in with the empirical literature on "intra-industry" trade. The work of Grubel and Lloyd (1975) is mentioned (Krugman 1979, p. 470).

It is argued in these articles that these ideas have not been given enough room in textbooks, and it is indirectly argued that at least one explanation for this is that these ideas have not been formalized in a convincing way. Krugman

(1979) writes that the hypothesis has been given little attention in formal trade theory (p. 469). In Krugman (1981) he writes "The purpose of this paper is to formalize one possible explanation of these seeming paradoxes" (p. 960).

In the 1980 article, he writes that his model "provides a formal justification for the commonly made argument that countries will tend to export those goods for which they have relatively large domestic markets" (Krugman 1980, p. 950). Krugman (1981) writes "What this paper does is put the argument in terms of a formal model, a step which may be of some help in clarifying and disseminating ideas which have been 'in the air' for some time" (p. 959).

The reason for why he builds a mathematical model seems to be primarily pragmatic. Given the rules of the game at the time, it was important for credibility to build a model in which the possible explanation of trade actually leads to trade.

8.3.2   The Characteristics of the Model

To fulfil this pragmatic aim, the models had to have certain characteristics. The models had to be relatively simple so the mechanism in question was easy to follow (see further below). The model had to have certain behavioural assumptions – utility maximizing consumers and profit maximizing firms. This is not motivated in the articles, but can also be seen as simply following "the rules of the game".

It was also important that the model was a general equilibrium model. This is not motivated either, but a reasonable interpretation is that if a model is a partial equilibrium model, then there might be forces that in a longer perspective changes the equilibrium. To be convincing, the model therefore had to be a general equilibrium model. Assumptions had also to be made about market structure, and Krugman uses a simple version of the standard model of monopolistic competition that was developed by Dixit and Stiglitz (1977).

The models in Krugman's three early articles are very good examples of what Mäki calls *isolation models*, as Krugman assumes away all the factors that explain trade in the classical and dominating theories: there are no differences between countries in factors of production or technology, and there are no comparative advantages between the two countries in the model. It would, however, be rather strange to call the model *a credible world* when a number of very important factors are excluded from the model (see further below about what the model is said to accomplish). The term isolation model seems more clarifying.

8.3.3   Simplifications Made

In a large number of places in the early articles, Krugman emphasizes that there are a lot of special and unrealistic assumptions in the models. Here are some examples of formulations from these articles. Krugman (1979, p. 470) writes that:

> Instead of trying to develop a general model, this model will assume particular forms for the utility and cost functions. The functional forms chosen give the model a simplified structure that makes the analysis easier.

In the 1980 article, he writes "in this paper a somewhat more restrictive formulation of demand is used to make the analysis in later sections easier" (Krugman 1980, p. 950). In the 1981 article he writes "It must be emphasized that the model presented here is in no sense a general one" (Krugman 1981, p. 960). When comparing with an earlier study, Krugman (1981, p. 967) writes "the virtue of this model is not in the difference of its conclusions but in the clarity with which they emerge."

Some of the assumptions are, however, claimed to be rather realistic. Krugman (1979), for example, writes "This assumption, which might alternatively be stated as an assumption that the elasticity of demand rises when the price of a good is increased, seems plausible".

8.3.4   An Example of "Pure Theory"

Building and analysing a simplified mathematical general equilibrium model can also be described as a work of "pure theory". Krugman (1981, p. 971) writes:

> In addition to helping make sense of some puzzling empirical results, this paper is, I hope, of some interest from the standpoint of pure theory. The model dispenses with the two most fundamental assumptions of standard trade theory: perfect competition and constant returns to scale. ... While the model depends on extremely restrictive assumptions, it does show that it is possible for trade theory to make at least some progress into this virtually unexplored territory.

8.3.5   And the Need for Generalization

In several places in the articles, he also discusses possible generalizations and, for example, mentions that one of the questionable assumptions has been replaced in another model – a model that, however, is more difficult to work with (Krugman 1980, p. 953). In Krugman (1980) there is a special section on "Generalizations and Extensions" (p. 958). Krugman (1981) says "These results may appear to depend crucially on the assumptions of this model, but in qualitative terms they can survive a good deal of generalization" (p. 967).

8.3.6   What the Analysis Accomplishes

An interesting question, given the discussions in the earlier chapters, is what the analysis of the models is claimed to accomplish. There is a number of formulations in the articles related to this.

Krugman (1979, p. 477):

> The important point to be gained from this analysis is that economies of scale can be shown to give rise to trade and gains from trade even when there are no international differences in tastes, technology, or factor endowments.

In the Summary and Conclusions section he writes (Krugman 1979, p. 479):

> [The paper] shows that trade need not be the result of international differences in technology or factor endowments.

But it is not really clear why it is important to show this, given that a number of simplifications are made, if the aim is to convince the scientific community that economies of scale are an important explanation for trade. Why should other economists care when the models are so simplified? The following formulation gives a hint about this:

> This paper shows that a clear, rigorous, and one hopes persuasive model of trade under conditions of increasing returns to scale can be constructed. Perhaps this will help economies of scale to a more prominent place in trade theory. (Krugman 1979, p. 479)

The formulation "persuasive model" indicates that a good model is a model that is seen as a good model by the leading actors in the field. And given the breakthrough of Krugman's theory it could be concluded that a persuasive model at the time was a model with the characteristics described above (maximizing agents, general equilibrium, a well-known market structure).

There are a number of formulations with rather weak claims like the ones that we have met in earlier chapters. (The italics below are added by me.) In the 1980 article he writes that the model "can *shed some light* on some issues which cannot be handled in more conventional models" (Krugman 1980, p. 950) and that "The analysis in this section has *obviously been suggestive* rather than conclusive. It relies heavily on very special assumptions and on the analysis of special cases". Krugman (1981) writes "This paper develops a simple model which *illustrates* this argument" (p. 959) and "What this paper does is put the argument in terms of a formal model, a step which *may be of some help in clarifying and disseminating ideas* which has been "in the air" for some time" (p. 959).

But there are also stronger formulations. Krugman (1980) also writes, "Nonetheless, the analysis does seem to *confirm* the idea that, in the presence of increasing returns, countries will tend to export the goods for which they have a large domestic market" (p. 958). In the 1981 article he writes:

> It must be emphasized that the model presented here is in no sense a general one. … Thus the results of the analysis are at best suggestive. Nonetheless, they *seem intuitively plausible and also seem to have something to do with actual experience.* (Krugman 1981, p. 960)

8.3.7   Comments About the Early Articles in the Nobel Prize Motivations

In the Nobel Prize texts on the scientific background to the prize to Krugman, the Nobel Prize Committee underline the contribution in the form of a formalized analysis within the framework of a general-equilibrium model. Neary (2009, p. 220) writes that Krugman "introduced probably the simplest possible fully-specified general-equilibrium model in which intra-industry trade could be rigorously demonstrated".

The Nobel Prize Committee also argues that it was Paul Krugman who most clearly and forcefully articulated the revolutionary nature of this new approach for the theory of international trade.

Above, I argued that the building of a general equilibrium model, and showing that trade can arise in such a model without the classical factors behind trade, was motivated by the rules of the game at the time. Showing that the relation holds in such a model was believed by Krugman to be the most efficient strategy to get other economist to take the ideas seriously. This is also in line with the comment from Krugman quoted at the end of the previous chapter in the context of Williamson's view on model-building. The Nobel Prize committee does, however, also write that:

> Such a framework is a prerequisite for systematic empirical work.

This argument cannot be found in any of Krugman's works that I have looked at, and not in Neary's comments. In the study of the AER-articles presented in earlier chapters, most of the empirical studies did not refer explicitly to any specific formalized framework, so the statement by the Nobel Prize Committee about the relations between mathematical models of the isolation type and empirical studies seems to lack support.

8.4   LATER DEVELOPMENTS OF THE MODELS

When philosophers of Economics discuss models, they typically focus on a small number of classical articles, for example Schelling's segregation model or Akerlof's market for lemons model. These articles fit nicely into the category "isolation models", where a number of important factors are assumed away and where the focus is on one specific mechanism.

The text from the Nobel Prize Committee gives an interesting picture of scientific development where an initially very simple model is developed in a number of different directions. It is not obvious that the term "isolation model" is a good description of the models that are built during later stages of the development of a theoretical model. After presenting the basic structure of Krugman's early articles the committee writes:

> Building on Krugman's analysis, a vast literature has developed exploring the implications of returns to scale and monopolistic competition for trade patterns in richer model settings.

The development is, somewhat simplified, of two different types. The first is to investigate the robustness of the result in the isolation model and the second is to integrate the new mechanism in models that – in this case – include the classical factors that explain trade.

8.4.1   Checking the Robustness of the Simple Model

Already in Krugman's own articles several robustness issues are investigated, for example what happens if transport cost are introduced, if migration between countries is allowed, if there are differences between countries in preferences or in the size of the country's labour force? He also discusses introducing some differences in production technology between the countries. As mentioned above, he claims that the results, at least in qualitative terms "can survive a good deal of generalization" (Krugman 1981, p. 967)

In the book "Market structure and foreign trade: Increasing returns, imperfect competition, and the international economy" by Helpman and Krugman (1985), the authors, for example, investigate what happens if the assumption about market structure is changed. They construct models of contestable markets and Cournot oligopoly beside models with the earlier assumption about monopolistic competition. In the introduction they also write "At some point ... it becomes necessary that we attempt a synthesis that defines the common element in the variety of new models and at the same time reestablishes some continuity with older traditions" (Helpman and Krugman 1985, p. 1). In the early models there were both assumptions about imperfect competition and increasing returns to scale. In their book they also analyse the effects of these two assumptions separately (Chapters 4 and 5) and also look at alternative models of product differentiation (Chapter 6ff).

8.4.2 Integrating the New Idea in Models Including the Standard Factors

On this point the Nobel Prize Committee writes:

> Integrated models of inter industry trade (based on technology gaps and Heckscher-Ohlin differences in factor proportions) and intra-industry trade in differentiated goods (based on increasing returns to scale and monopolistic competition) were provided by Lancaster (1980), Dixit and Norman (1980), Krugman (1981) and, with greater generality, by Helpman (1981) and Helpman and Krugman (1985). Integration of the new and old trade theory was particularly important as it led to testable predictions about cross-country differences in trade patterns.

It can be interesting to look a little closer at Helpman (1981) and Helpman and Krugman (1985) from the perspective of model development in the relatively early stages of the development of a specific theory.

Helpman (1981) starts from the classical Heckscher–Ohlin model where trade is driven by differences in factor proportion. That model gives a number of predictions, for example that relative factor prices can be used to predict the kind of goods that are traded. Helpman describes the new analysis as a *generalization of the Heckscher–Ohlin theory*. He wants to construct a model that included both the traditional inter-sectoral trade and the new ideas about intra-sectoral trade, where Krugman is one author referred to. In the integrated model he can investigate whether the new more inclusive theory/model has the same implications as the old one. As he included both inter-sectoral and intra-sectoral trade, he can also investigate what determines the share of the different types of trade.

To simplify, he concludes that some of the traditional relations do not hold unless the utility and production functions fulfils certain rather restrictive conclusion (Helpman 1981, p. 329, p. 335). He also shows that the size of the income differences between the countries will affect the share of intra-sectoral trade. The article ends with a section about empirical implications and Helpman also mentions an empirical study where the result of the study is consistent with the prediction about the determinants of the share of intra-industry trade.

Helpman and Krugman (1985) also analyse models with both traditional factor differences and models with economies of scale. They write:

> In general, however, the models developed in this book support a basic view in which trade patterns reflect comparative advantages plus additional specialization to realize scale economies. (Helpman and Krugman 1985, p. 262)

The book furthermore underlines that the gains from trade increase when scale economies are taken into account, and Helpman and Krugman (1985) write "Our method of analysis in this book has been to derive sufficient conditions for gains from trade under alternative assumptions about market structure". But they end with the kind of guarded statement that we have met earlier in this book: "Our analysis in this book then *suggests an overall presumption* that..." (Helpman and Krugman 1985, p. 265, my emphasis).

8.5   EMPIRICAL STUDIES AND TESTS

The Nobel Prize Committee mentions some early empirical studies and here is a summary of them.

Helpman (1987) uses data from 14 industrial countries to test some of the direct implications of the simple models that Krugman and Helpman had presented. These implications concern, for example, that intra-industrial trade will grow when GDP increases and that the share of intra-industry trade will be higher when the GDPs of the countries are rather similar. In the introduction he writes: "Although the success of the new models in explaining stylized facts is encouraging, it is very desirable to examine more carefully their consistency with the data" (Helpman 1987, p. 63). After doing this, his conclusion is that the data are consistent with the implications from the new models. He writes "These results are encouraging, in particular in view of the fact that we have used highly disaggregated data" (Helpman 1987, p. 80).

It is also argued that for a theory to be interesting it is not enough that it "fits the data", it should also matter from a welfare and policy perspective. Harris (1984) is interested in the effect of trade liberalization and asks whether the effects of trade liberalization are different in a model where there are economies of scale and product differentiation compared with the traditional models. He builds models that include different trade-influencing factors and calibrates the different models on Canadian data. The final step is to investigate if the effects of trade liberalization differ between the models, and Harris shows that this is the case and that trade liberalization increases welfare more in models with economies of scale and product differentiation. He also concludes that:

> It is evident the conventional model and the industrial organization model give significantly different views on the pattern of interindustry adjustment to trade. (Harris 1984, p. 1030)

> To ignore these features, if it is known a priori they are significant at the industry level, is to seriously misspecify the general equilibrium analysis. (Harris 1984, p. 1018)

> It is both feasible and useful to incorporate industrial organization features in applied general equilibrium models. (Harris 1984, p 1031)

Empirical studies of an object with a chaos-theoretical structure are always problematic and seldom gives full and conclusive support to a theory. Leamer and Levinsohn (1995) point to some problems, for example in Helpman (1987) and also in later studies. The typical problem is that the size of the parameters estimated depended on the exact specification of the models and that the relations may not be robust to changes in these specifications. Given some specifications, the theory gets little support (Leamer and Levinsohn 1995, p. 1381). They also note that the empirical implications are not strictly derived from the theoretical models (Leamer and Levinsohn 1995, p. 1379) and that Helpman should have discussed alternative theories that could explain the observed empirical relations. Implicit in the Nobel Prize Committee motivations is that no convincing competing theory about intra-industry trade has been presented.

A later empirical study, also mentioned by the Nobel Prize Committee, is Antweiler and Trefler (2002) and this also exemplifies a development where the new theory is combined with the older theories into a more integrated theory. Their primary goal is "to quantify the extent of increasing returns to scale in the context of a general-equilibrium model of international trade" (p. 93). They are using a large database with many countries and many sectors and five years between 1972 and 1992. As always, a number of assumptions have to be made when building a general equilibrium model, which it is possible to estimate (these are summarized on Antweiler and Trefler 2002, p. 102). In the Conclusions they write:

> our empirical result strikingly demonstrate that scale economies must figure prominently for any understanding of the factor content of trade … Our results point to the importance of integrating constant- and increasing-returns-to scale industries within a single general-equilibrium framework. (Antweiler and Trefler 2002, p. 112)

8.6   CONCLUDING COMMENTS

This case study shows that the following steps can be identified in the process of getting a new theory accepted.

- An anomaly is observed. In this case the large share of intra-industry trade.
- An idea/hypothesis/theory about what can explain the anomaly. In this case economies of scale, heterogenous preferences and low transportation cost.
- The idea "seems reasonable" with a clear logic behind the hypothesis and there is no obvious counterarguments to the idea.
- The idea is formalized in a very simple general equilibrium model. The result is rather robust, and no one is able to find any questionable crucial assumptions in the models. The model analysis indicates that the anomaly *can* be explained by the proposed idea/hypothesis/theory.
- No one is able to formulate a competing credible hypothesis for the explanation of the anomaly.
- The new theory can be integrated in models that also include earlier explanatory factors. In these more inclusive models, the new theory leads to new predictions that can be tested empirically.
- Different types of empirical studies are carried out and – all in all – give support to the new theory. The results strongly suggest that the new ideas should not be neglected either when mathematical models are built or when empirical studies are carried out. Given the chaos-like structure of the object under study it is not seen as a big problem that some of the empirical tests do not give strong support to the theory.

From the perspective of the philosophy of Economics, one important observation in this chapter is that the *mathematical models can play different roles in different stages of the development of a theory*. If the aim of the model-builder is only to show that a certain mechanism *might* explain an anomaly then an isolation model works fine. But the next step is to integrate the new mechanism in a model that also include the traditional mechanism. The model is still simplified but it does not focus on one specific explanation/mechanism and it should therefore no longer be called an isolation model. This integration makes it possible to see how the new assumptions affect the implications in a situation where the earlier mechanisms are also at work. The researcher compares the implications of the old models with the implications of a model that includes both the old and the new mechanisms. These implications can the tested empirically. Testing the implications of the isolation model is not as interesting, as everyone knows that the model leaves out other mechanisms that are important for what happens in the economy. In order to test the theory, there is a need to build models that try to integrate different mechanisms and make it possible to compare their importance.

9. Summary and implications

9.1 SUMMARY OF MAIN RESULTS

If you want to understand the role of theories and models in Economics it is necessary to have some preliminaries. The first of these – discussed in Chapter 2 – is what kind of object a science studies, as that will determine what is possible to accomplish. My hypothesis was that Economics studies a chaos-theoretic object: the economy is a complex system with many interacting parts, and where relatively small differences in the characteristics of the system will affect how it will react to various changes. It should also be added that it is a system that changes over time.

If this is true, we should expect that there will be differences in what Nobel Prize winners in Economics have done compared with what prize winners in Physics (where at least large parts are not studying chaos-theoretic objects) have done. The empirical study presented in Chapter 2 supports these implications, for example that theories in Economics more often were described as frameworks and that no Nobel Prize winner in Economics has received the prize for finding a stable empirical regularity. Mathematics cannot, in a science that studies a chaos-theoretic objects, describe empirical laws, so one use of mathematics instead is to create model economies and investigate what relations hold in these models. The hypothesis is that investigating what happens in such models can help us understand how the world works.

The next step in the study here, concerned what economists really do in their research. From the Nobel Prize motivations, several different types of path-breaking contributions could be identified (Chapter 3). There were traditional normal-scientific contributions such as improving existing methods or coming up with a new idea that can explain anomalies in a specific field. It could also be the introduction of new methods, from the early prize winners that started the mathematization of economic theory to late winners that introduced laboratory and field experiments in a systematic way. There were, however, also "mini-revolutions" that affected a large part of Economics, without replacing fundamental features of the research strategy. The introduction of rational expectations, transaction cost, information problems and game theory led to such large-scale changes in Economics, according to the motivations of the Nobel Prize Committee. Replacing simple maximization assumption with behavioural assumptions more grounded in psychological and sociological research could be seen as another such mini-revolution, even if it is not described in that way by the committee.

Chapter 4 focused on ordinary scientific articles published in the leading journal *American Economic Review* in 1990 and 2020. The following types of studies were identified: (1) the "theoretical" economists build mathematical models and analyse relations in these models; (2) "pure" empirical studies that do not have a specific model or theory as a starting point; and (3) studies that include both a mathematical model and empirical study that typically are used to estimate/calibrate the model so it can be used for explaining and predicting the effects of different policies and calculating welfare effects.

Focusing on the "theoretical" studies, their typical structure is the following. They start with some kind of problem in existing models in relation to some empirical observations. A new model is needed to explain a phenomenon and the new model is in some respect more realistic than earlier models. These additions or adjustments in the model make it possible to explain the anomaly. In the conclusions, the researcher typically returns to the real-world situation. The conclusions are formulated in a number of different ways, but are typically rather guarded. It is common to say that what was proved in the model *can* explain the real-world phenomena, that the analysis *suggests* or *indicates* that a certain mechanism explains the observed phenomena. The analysis in the model *throws light on* or *highlights* a certain feature that can be important.

There are almost no claims that results from the study can be generalized, which is what we would expect if the researchers study a chaos-theoretic object. There were, however, often claims that the study showed that a certain new aspect should not be neglected in future studies and that some methodological improvements made in the study could be useful in future studies.

Both from the study of Nobel Prize motivations and the study of articles in *American Economic Review* it is clear that the aim of research is to understand how the world works, even though logical implications or logically necessary conditions sometimes can be interesting on their own.

Chapter 5 shows that it is hard to fit the development of Economics into Kuhn's theory of paradigms and scientific revolutions, where there is a radical shift in assumptions/theories and approaches during a rather short period of time. It seems more correct to see economics at a certain period of time as consisting of a number of components that can be changed, one by one, without changing the rest of the structure. New methods, such as laboratory and field experiments, can be added without replacing earlier methods. Certain assumptions in traditional theories/models can be replaced, for example when behavioural assumptions are changed, without changing established methods. New perspectives can also be added, for example transaction cost and asymmetric information, while the general research strategy is the same.

In Chapter 6 there is an attempt to take a more holistic view on the use of the words "theory" and "theoretical" in Economics. It is pointed out that a number of distinctions have to be made and the most important is between a theory as a general framework without any specific empirical hypotheses, and a theory that simply is a hypothesis about what can explain a specific observation. A framework introduces concepts and approaches and points out possible explanations.

Theoretical studies in economics nowadays means the same as a study where the core is an analysis of a mathematical model, as is discussed further in Chapter 7. The study of the AER articles showed that the word "theory"/"theoretical" (and "hypothesis") are used rather sparsely. It was furthermore found that the "theoretical" articles seldom ended with saying that the next step is to test the theory, and also that the empirical studies seldom started with references to specific theories, models or theory-related hypotheses. These gaps between studies where a mathematical model is the core and empirical studies seem to have increased over time.

Economists rather talk about building and investigating models instead of developing theory. They rather talk about estimating and measuring relations instead of testing a theory or a hypothesis. When broader implications of results are discussed in the 2020-articles, the results are typically related to earlier results in different "literatures", which perhaps is an indirect way of relating the results to earlier theories/hypothesis.

Chapter 7 focuses on models, and the first result was that the word "model"/"modelling" is used very frequently in all the different types of AER-articles. There are two main contexts where the word is used. The first is the "theoretical" models where the core of the article is the construction and analysis of relations in a mathematical model, and the second use of "models" is when model refers to an econometric/statistical model that is formulated and estimated in (some) empirical articles.

In this book, the focus is on what is called theoretical models and in earlier chapters it has been shown that the aim of such a study is to explain something and, for example, suggest a possible cause of some anomaly that has been observed. The conclusion is often formulated as that the analysis suggests or indicates that a certain factor is the cause.

In the general philosophical literature about models, it is pointed out that models in science can have many purposes. It can, for example, be claimed that the model is good for pedagogical purposes, as an illustration of an idea/mechanism, as a starting point for constructing more realistic models or that the model is a good approximation of a certain real situation/process/market. This means that a model cannot be analysed in isolation. One must also look at the claims made about the model in a certain text. The claims made can change over time and vary between researchers even if the model is the same.

It is suggested that the models in the Type 1 articles that aim at increasing our knowledge of how a real economy works can be analysed with a Bayesian framework. The result that certain relations hold in a specific model-economy is then seen as new information, and the next question is how much it is rational to change the probability of certain empirical statements given this new information. As pointed out in the philosophy of Economics literature, the model that is presented in an article is typically accompanied by a "commentary". Besides making the purpose and claim clearer, this commentary can discuss how good an approximation certain assumptions are, how robust the relations proven are, and the commentary can include a comparisons with competing hypotheses. This commentary is important for judging how much it is rational to change the probability of specific empirical statements given the proven relation in the model. An important observation is that how much it is rational to change the probability of the empirical claim will not only depend on the characteristics of the specific model (how "good an approximation" it is) but also on the availability of competing credible models.

A case study of Paul Krugman's New Trade Theory is presented in Chapter 8 and illustrates how a theory can come to be generally accepted. The following steps were identified. (1) An anomaly is observed. (2) An idea/hypothesis/ theory about what can explain the anomaly is put forward. (3) The new idea "seems reasonable" with a clear logic behind the hypothesis. No obvious counterarguments to the idea can be found. (4) The idea can be formalized in a very simple general equilibrium model. The results in the first simple models are rather robust to changes in assumptions, and no one is able to find any questionable and crucial assumptions in the models. (5) No one is able to formulate a competing credible hypothesis that can explain the anomaly. (6) The new theory can be integrated in models that also include earlier explanatory factors. In these more inclusive models, the new theory leads to new predictions that can be tested empirically. (7) Different types of empirical studies give support to the implications from the new theory.

9.2   CONCLUDING REFLECTIONS (1): ABOUT A PHILOSOPHY OF ECONOMICS

I think that this book illustrates the fruitfulness of discussing methodological questions with a clear empirical base. Methodological views should have implications that can be tested against different types of empirical material. In this book, this material was primarily Nobel Prize motivations and all full-length articles published in *American Economic Review* between 1990 and 2020. Looking closer at such empirical material can also generate new hypotheses and observations that are inconsistent with some established views about theory and models.

One observation, especially from the Krugman case study, was that the "theoretical" mathematical models can have different roles in different stages of the development of a theory. In a first stage it can be correct to call the models "isolation models". The model focuses on one mechanism that can produce a certain result and leaves out other mechanisms. However, in later stages other types of models are built, both models that check the robustness of the results by changing different assumptions and models that tries to integrate the new theory and earlier theories in the same model.

In earlier chapters it was also seen that adding a feature to existing models was a common type of contribution, and calling this new somewhat more complex model an isolation model may not be the best description.

I have argued that one way of structuring the thinking about such models (and also other types of studies) is to use an informal Bayesian structure, and to analyse the result of a specific study in the same way as a court evaluates evidence. The direct result of the analysis, for example that certain things happen in a specific model, can be seen as new information, and the question then becomes how much it is rational to change the probability of specific empirical statements. This type of analysis has in the methodological literature been called "the commentary" by Mäki. My study has shown that such a commentary, for example, discusses the reasonableness of the assumptions in the model, how robust the results are, but also if there are specific empirical observations that support the hypothesis that the mechanism in the model is important in a specific real market.

An important implication of using such an informal Bayesian framework is that a model cannot be evaluated in isolation – for example by looking at how realistic specific assumptions are and if certain less realistic assumptions are harmless or crucial. A mechanism proposed in a certain model must be evaluated in the light of competing hypotheses. A certain model may seem very credible, but if there are other models with competing hypothesis that also seem credible, it is not possible to draw any empirical conclusions from the fact that the relation exists in a credible model. An example is given in the next section.

9.3 CONCLUDING REFLECTIONS (2): ABOUT METHODS IN ECONOMICS

Economists have a difficult task as they study an object that has a chaos-theoretic structure – a statement that was supported by the evidence presented in Chapter 2 where Nobel Prize motivations in Economics were compared with the motivations in Physics. The researcher in Economics cannot assume that the same mechanisms are at work, and that a phenomenon has (exactly) the same explanation, when discussing similar events at different times or in different places. This also means that one should not expect to find any precise and stable quantitative relations – and no Nobel Prizes were ever awarded for that. Generalizations from one time/place to another will be questionable, and it is not surprising that such claims cannot be found in the material investigated.

When studying such a complex and constantly evolving object, one should expect that researchers are rather guarded in their final conclusions. The empirical study of articles showed that it was common to have formulations that the results *indicted* or *suggested* something or *threw light* on something and that (at least) a certain (new) factor should not be neglected in future studies.

When studying a chaos-theoretic object there is a need for a conceptual/theoretical framework to structure problems and find possible answers, and also for models that illustrate various possible mechanism and explanatory factors. Most economists would probably agree that Microeconomic theory, Contract theory and Game theory are important such frameworks.

It is not easy to find any clear and easily applied criteria for evaluating conceptual frameworks. One thinks of Kuhn's idea that people that work within different paradigms live in different worlds and that paradigms/frameworks cannot be compared. I am not sure that this is correct, but it is obviously more difficult to "test" a conceptual framework than a specific statement referring to a specific time and place. I am, however, an optimist in the sense that I believe that if two people using two different conceptual frameworks really want to evaluate the value of framework X and framework Y in relation to the purpose Z, they could come a long way towards results such as, "If you want to investigate problems of type P then conceptual framework C1 is probably better to use that conceptual framework C2". Evaluating this optimistic hypothesis is however not easy either![1]

My final view is that when studying a chaos-theoretic object such as an economy, *one should not throw away any kind of information*. A lot of things can be helpful when trying to understand, for example, how a specific market works. Interviews, articles in business journals, information from people you happen to know, government documents, questionnaires, statistical analysis of "hard" data, laboratory experiments, field experiments, participatory observation but also introspection. From a Bayesian perspective one should look for the information and make the kind of study that could lead to the largest changes in the estimated probability of the relevant empirical statements.

---

[1]   In the 1970s I wrote (in Swedish) a Master's thesis in theoretical philosophy about the concept of presupposition. There, I argued that it should be possible – if people were interested – to unveil and evaluate presuppositions behind different statements – and the presuppositions behind these presuppositions. It could at least not be shown that such a conversion would be impossible!

There might be diminishing marginal returns to a specific scientific activity in relation to a specific problem. An old example is Blinder and Choi's (1990) article "A shred of evidence on theories of wage stickiness". There were, at the time, a number of competing models/hypotheses about wage stickiness, and what Blinder and Choi did was to interview a number of people working with wage-setting in companies. In this case, the marginal utility of building more theoretical/mathematical models might have been small, while the possible marginal utility of interviewing people who were working with these issues could be large. The interviews can give information about how reasonable specific assumptions are.

But it can, of course, also be the other way around: there might exist empirical information without any clear structure and then the marginal utility of building a series of small mathematical models might be high. Krugman's articles where he launched the New Trade Theory seems to be an example of this.

One underlying issue is how much one needs to know about the institutional detail in order to build an interesting mathematical model. Williamson's idea, described in Chapter 7, was that constructing mathematical models should be done at a rather late stage of the research process, if the aim is to help us understand how a specific market works. But I would rather argue that we can, in all stages, have use for both mathematical models and institutional information.

All the possible methods mentioned above can also help us get new ideas and find out complications in existing explanations. Rodrik (2015) underlines that working with mathematical models can show that it was not so easy to prove a certain relation as expected. A lot of specific and maybe not so credible assumptions had to be made to make the model work and the relation proved. This type of problem indicates that other factors might be important in a convincing explanation. But similar things can, in my experience, happen when you interview an experienced person working in a specific field. They point out complications in your theories and mentions aspects that you had not thought about before.

It is, however, hard to measure the marginal utility of different types of studies in a certain situation. In the 1980s, I was active in the Left Party of Sweden and, at that time, there were always heated discussions about the usefulness of parliamentary versus non-parliamentary work. At one party conference I requested the floor – I seldom did that – and said that as it is very difficult to know what an efficient strategy is, then the rational strategy must be that each member does what they think is most meaningful and/or most fun. I cannot say that I got much support for this view, but I feel roughly the same about methods in Economics. Do what you are good at, do what you think is fun – but do not argue that the method you work with in general is better than other strategies. Everything is problematic when you study a chaos-theoretic object!

9.4　CONCLUDING REFLECTIONS (3): BACK TO MCCLOSKEY

As mentioned in the introduction, I owe McCloskey and large debt, and therefore it should be fair to conclude with some reflections on (primarily) her latest books. But let us first return to the classical article "The rhetoric of economics" (McCloskey 1983). Important points that are also related to some of the observations made earlier in this book are the following:

> Economists in fact argue on wider grounds, and should. Their genuine, workaday rhetoric, the way they argue inside their heads or their seminar rooms, diverges from the official rhetoric. Economists should become more self-conscious about their rhetoric, because they will then better know why they agree or disagree. (McCloskey 1983, p. 482)

> Economists can do better if they will look soberly at the varieties of their arguments. (McCloskey 1983, p. 499)

We saw in the section about "The commentary" in Chapter 7 that there were references to all kinds of material when the economist wanted to argue for the relevance of the new factors included in the specific model. But I have also complained, for example in relation to some statements made by Rodrik, that there were no real discussions about how to evaluate whether a certain model includes mechanisms that are important or not.

In one of the two recent books (*Bettering Humanomics: A New, and Old, Approach to Economic Science* (McCloskey 2021) one can read (p. xii):

> A future economics should ... use the available scientific log and evidence, all of it – experimental, simulative, introspective, questionnaire, graphical, categorical, statistical, literary, historical, psychological, sociological, political, aesthetic, ethical.

This is of course similar to my statement above that when studying a chaos-theoretic object all methods are problematic and therefore one should not throw away any sources of informational.

It is however interesting to see that McCloskey reaches her conclusion through a very different route. Her starting point is how to explain "The great enrichment": the fact that average income has increased dramatically over the last centuries. She presents counterarguments to, for example, theories that argue that this development can be explained by institutions and incentives. Instead, she argues that certain ethical views and a certain rhetoric played a crucial role. The heading of one of the chapters in the book is "The dignity of liberalism did it" (McCloskey 2021, p. 59f)

If one accepts that view that ideas, ethical beliefs and a certain rhetoric played an important role, then it is necessary to use sources where it is possible to get information about what these beliefs are and the rhetoric that dominates society at a certain point in time. And then of course a broader set of sources would be needed to collect the relevant information, including for example newspapers and literary works from the specific period where arguments that were seen as persuasive could be found. In Economics, researchers need a broader empirical base, this should also be reflected in doctoral programmes, see McCloskey (2022, pp. 71ff.) for some suggestions.

McCloskey also writes "Good science – good social science most obviously – is made by good, honest, open-minded, liberal people, or else it is likely to break bad" (McCloskey 2022, p viii). When I read this, I came to think about a statement by Ian Hacking in the book "Representing and intervening: Introductory topics in the philosophy of science" where he argued that progress in the natural sciences needed a mix of people. He wrote:

> What is so great about science is that it is a collaboration between different kinds of people.
> The remarkable fact about recent physical sciences is that it creates a new, collective, human artifact by giving full range to three fundamental human interests, speculation, calculation and experiment. (Hacking 1983, p 248)

Thinking in Kuhnian terms, maybe a fruitful collaboration that leads to scientific development needs a balance between five types of researchers: (1) those who rather single-mindedly argue for major changes in current theories and methods; (2) those who also rather single-mindedly fight for the current mainstream; (3) mediators who try to find a common ground among the views of these more single-minded people (one task for McCloskey's liberals?); and (4) researchers who work with specific economic problems and either (a) just work with the dominating methods or (b) who are more pragmatic and simply use the methods that seems best and do not worry so much about what is established or not.

Appendix: Information about the empirical studies

A1   THE NOBEL PRIZE STUDIES

About the Nobel Prize and Earlier Studies

As written in Alfred Nobel's will from 1895, he gave most of his wealth to a foundation that every year should give out prizes in physics, chemistry, medicine, literature and a peace prize. The physics prize was given the first time in 1901. In 1968, The Swedish Riksbank (Sweden's central bank) established what is formally called the "Prize in Economic Sciences in Memory of Alfred Nobel" through a donation on the bank's 300th anniversary. On the website of the Riksbank it is written that: "The prize is awarded every year to a person or persons in the field of economic sciences who have produced work of outstanding importance". The procedure for selecting the winner of the Economics prize is the same as for other prizes (see Lindbeck 1985, 2001). There is a Prize Committee with six members selected by and from the Swedish Academy of Sciences. The committee presents a recommendation, and the Academy makes the final decision.

Over the years there have been various criticisms of the Nobel Prize in Economics (see for example Luyendijk 2015). Is Economics really a science comparable to physics and chemistry? And why is there no prize in other social sciences? Does the prize imply that Economics is seen as more scientific than other social sciences? Is the selection of winners more based on ideological preferences than scientific contributions? Several of these issues are discussed in the book *The Nobel Factor: The Prize in Economics, Social Democracy, and the Market Turn* (Offer & Söderberg 2016) and partly also in Karier (2010), even though the purpose of the latter book primarily is to present the contributions of the laureates for a broader audience.

The aim of this book is, however, neither to evaluate the scientific status of Economics (compared with other sciences) nor to evaluate the "real" contributions of specific Nobel Prize winners. Even if there is an ideological bias in the selection of the winners, the economists that are given the prize can be assumed to have done something that differs from what other economists with the same ideology have done. The winners have made something that is seen as more important – and this makes it relevant to look at the contributions of the winners.

Chowdhury (2012) looks at the first 41 years, but beside a classification of the fields studied, he focuses on where laurates come from (countries and universities). In my study, one aim is instead to look for the type of contributions made. In general, one can say that I do not study the Nobel Prize as such, but use material published by the Nobel Committee to investigate some more specific questions.

The Data

The study is based on the first 50 years of the Economics prize (1969–2018). Only Physics prizes for these years have been studied. The material used are the following official documents presented by the Nobel Foundation, and these documents are all available from the website of the Nobel Foundation. The same types of documents are presented by the foundation for all sciences.

1. A short motivation: a one sentence motivation of why the winner was awarded the prize. This is available for all the 50 years covered in the study (1969–2018).
2. A press release. From 1972, a press release with around 1000 words has been published, but since the year 2000, when the Academy started to publish a special document with information to the public, the press releases have become shorter (around 350 words).
3. The speech by the representative of the academy at the award ceremony. This is also available for every year, and there are some variations in length, but typically is around 1000 words.
4. 'Information for the public'. This special document was first published in the year 2000 and it is usually a 4–5 page document.
5. "Advanced information". This special document has been published since 1995 and is typically 20–50 pages. This document was only studied for Economics and not used in the comparison between Economics and Physics.

In Economics, there is also one or several articles published in the *Scandinavian Journal of Economics* about the contributions of the laureate. These articles have also been studied and used where it seemed relevant. These articles are not used in the comparison between Economics and Physics and not in the quantitative studies. The articles from the *Scandinavian Journal of Economics* that have been used are included in the reference list.

Relevance

Using Nobel Prize motivations for comparing Economics and Physics and for studying contributions in a science has some obvious advantages. The motivations are available for a large number of years, while, for example, interviews can only be carried out with scientists that are currently alive or studied where there are published interviews. A further advantage is that the same type of material is available for both sciences. Journals might have different policies or there might be different traditions concerning what should be included in an article. The Nobel Prize texts are produced by a group of scientists every year, and that means that risks of bias related to a specific individual's views should be relatively small. There is no interviewer bias. Furthermore, the focus in the documents is on the contributions of specific scientists, and not on presenting an official view of the specific science. This means that the text could give a more concrete and correct picture of what is really done in the science, compared with direct interviews where the interviewee might be tempted to present what they think will be seen as a good view of the science in question. Even though the prize is awarded, and the texts are produced, by a specific scientific Academy in one country, the fact that the prize has very high status, indicates that the criteria used by the Swedish Academy for selecting laurates are respected by scientists around the world.

How the Tests were Carried Out

Most of the quantitative tests are based on word counts from (1) the press release, (2) the speech to the laureate when the prize is handed over, and (3) the popular information. Both the total number of occurrences and the number of years where the word being considered occur are studied, but the test focuses on the number of years where the word occurs. In one case the short motivations are also used. All occurrences have been checked and only occurrences related to the work of laureate are included and only "positive" occurrences. The word *explain* can, for example, be included both in statements that the aim of science is to explain, and in statements that the aim is not the explain.

Standard t-tests (without assuming the same variance) have been used for testing whether there are statistically significant differences at the 5 per cent level.

For the more qualitative tests the same texts have been used and in those cases the texts have been read several times looking for formulations related to the issue at hand. A number of quotations related to this were collected and are presented in the relevant sections. My belief is that another independent reader would find the same quotations relevant and draw the same conclusions.

All material used are publicly available and open to analysis by those who are sceptical of my interpretations.[1]

A2   THE STUDY OF ARTICLES IN *AMERICAN ECONOMIC REVIEW*

American Economic Review was chosen because it is a high-ranked journal without any specific focus concerning methods or topics. There is, however, one problem with this choice. A number of new journals were launched by the American Economic Association in 2009. It is of course hard to know if this has affected what is published in the main journal, but the assumption here is that the articles in the new journals have high quality, it not as high as the articles published in the main journal. An argument for this is that the new journals cover almost all areas of Economics (macroeconomics, microeconomic, applied economics and economic policy). It is therefore not the case that articles with a specific focus or a specific method are allocated to the new journals.

The goal was to have 100 full-length research articles, excluding articles with presidential addresses or Nobel lectures. As there were not enough articles in 1990, some articles from early issues in 1991 were included. In order to simplify the presentation, I will mention only the years 1990 and 2020 even though some articles are from 1991.

There are potential problems with looking at only one journal and two specific years, as the preferences of the editors may influence the types of articles published. The current study should therefore be seen more as an exploratory study. In order to draw more definite conclusions about patterns and trends, more journals and more years should be analysed.

The method used was to go through the articles with a specific question in mind and then make notes for each article. The first step was to make a broad classification of what is presented in the articles – what the researcher has actually done. More detailed questions were then formulated for each type of article; for example, what the more specific aim of the study was and the type of conclusions drawn. For each group of questions, the articles were checked one more time and notes and/or quotations were collected from each article. When a first version of the study was ready, the articles were checked one

---

[1]   I have collected the material in files to make analysis easier and these files are available from the author for anyone who wants to check the results presented. An Excel-file with the wordcount for each year for each specific hypothesis is also available from the author.

more time to see if anything should be added. Some minor additions and clarifications were made after this final check of the articles.

When changes over time were investigated, a t-test was used to check whether the changes were statistically significant (at the 5 per cent level).

A3 THE 1993 STUDY: "A CASE STUDY OF NORMAL SCIENCE IN THEORETICAL ECONOMICS"

In this study I focused on a single economist, the internationally respected Swedish theoretical economist Lars E. O. Svensson. He was, when the article was written, professor at the Institute for International Economic Studies at Stockholm University. The choice of a single economist can of course lead to a distorted view, but it must be remembered that the economist in question was chosen because he had many articles published in prestigious international journals where works are carefully refereed. The published articles had won the acclaim of others in the profession and should therefore tell us about more than what characterizes the work of a single economist

The study covers all published articles by L. E. O. Svensson from 1976 to 1986. This material consists of 36 articles, of which 22 were co-authored. A list of the articles can be found in the appendix to Lind (1993). The articles concern the following main fields:

A. Efficiency in intertemporal models (four articles).
B. Fix-price models and effective demand (two articles).
C. Balance-of-payment and effects of rising oil prices (eight articles).
D. Time-consistency of economic policy (two articles).
E. Monetary theory (cash-in-advance models) (four articles).
F. General trade theory (ten articles).
G. Others (six articles).

A4 THE 2007 STUDY "THE STORY AND THE MODEL DONE"

Eight articles published between 1997 and 2003 were studied in detail. They were found as a by-product of a broader literature search conducted for the article Lind (2003) and were selected because they concerned rent regulation and that the central part of the article was the construction and analysis of a mathematical model. The articles come from three leading American journals: *Regional Science and Urban Economics*, *The Journal of Real Estate*

Finance and Economics, and *Journal of Housing Economics*. The articles are listed below.

1. Anas, Alex (1997). Rent control with matching economies: A model of European housing market regulation. *Journal of Real Estate Finance and Economics*, 15(1), 111–137.
2. Heffley, Dennis (1998). Landlords, tenants and the public sector in a spatial equilibrium model of rent control. *Regional Science and Urban Economics*, 28, 745–772.
3. Skelley, Chris (1998). Rent control and complete contract equilibria. *Regional Science and Urban Economics*, 28, 711–743.
4. Arnott, Richard and Igarashi, Masahiro (2000). Rent control, mismatch costs and search efficiency. *Regional Science and Urban Economics*, 30, 249–288.
5. Iwata, Shinichiro (2002). The Japanese Tenant Protection Law and asymmetric information on tenure length. *Journal of Housing Economics*, 11, 125–151.
6. McFarlane, Alastair (2003). Rent stabilization and the long-run supply of housing. *Regional Science and Urban Economics*, 33, 305–333.
7. Seshimo, Hiroyuki (2003). Optimal tenant protection. *Regional Science and Urban Economics*, 33, 59–92.
8. Raess, Pascal and von Ungern-Sternberg, Thomas (2002). A model of regulation in the rental housing market. *Regional Science and Urban Economics*, 32, 475–500.

References

Angrist, J., Azoulay, P., Ellison, G., Hill, R., and Feng-Lu, S. (2017). Economic research evolves: Fields and styles. *American Economic Review: Papers & Proceedings*, 107(5), 293–297

Antweiler, W. and Trefler, D. (2002). Increasing returns and all that: A view from trade, *American Economic Review*, 92, 93–119.

Backhouse, R. and Cherrier, B. (2017). The age of the applied economist: The transformation of economics since the 1970s. *History of Political Economy*, 49 (Supplement): 1–33.

Balassa, B. (1967). *Trade liberalization among industrial countries*. New York: McGraw-Hill.

Barberis, N. (2018). Richard Thaler and the rise of behavioral economics. *The Scandinavian Journal of Economics*, 120, 661–684.

Baumol, W. J. (1972). John R. Hicks' contribution to economics. *The Swedish Journal of Economics*, 74, 503–527.

Baumol, W. J. (1979). On the contribution of Herbert A. Simon to economics. *The Scandinavian Journal* of Economics, 81, 74–82.

Bird, A. (2014). *Thomas Kuhn*. Princeton, NJ: Princeton University Press. (First edition 2000.)

Blinder, A. and Choi, D. H. (1990). A shred of evidence on theories of wage stickiness. *Quarterly Journal of Economics*, 105(4), 1003-1001

Bohm, P. and Lind, H. (1993). Policy evaluation quality: A quasi-experimental study of regional employment subsidies in Sweden. *Regional Science and Urban Economics*, 23, 51–65.

Chowdury, A. (2012). The Nobel Prize in Economics: A reflection of the first 41 years, 1969-2009. *The Jahangirnagar Journal of Business Studies*, 1–20.

Colander, D. and Kupers, R. (2014). *Complexity and the art of public policy*. Princeton and Oxford: Princeton University Press.

Dahlman, C. (2018). *Beviskraft: Metod för bevisvärdering i brottmål.* (*Power of evidence: Method for evaluation of evidence in criminal cases*). Stockholm: Norstedts juridik.

Devlin W. J. and Bokulich, A. (eds) (2015). *Kuhn's Structure of scientific revolutions – 50 years On*. Boston Studies in the Philosophy and History of Science. New York: Springer.

Dixit, A. K. and Norman, V. (1980). *Theory of international trade: A dual, general equilibrium approach*. London: Cambridge University Press.

Dixit, A. K. and Stiglitz, J. E. (1977). Monopolistic competition and optimum product diversity. *American Economic Review*, 67, 297–308.

Dolfsma, W. and Welch P. J. (2009). Paradigms and novelty in Economics: The history of economic thought as a source of enlightenment. *The American Journal of Economics and Sociology*, 68, 1085–1106.

Donaldson, D. (2022). Blending theory and data: A Space Odyssey. *Journal of Economic Perspectives*, 36 (3), 185-210.

Favereau, J. and Nagatsu, M. (2020). Holding back from theory: Limits and methodological alternatives of randomized field experiments in development economics. *Journal of Economic Methodology*, 27(3), 191–211.

Gibbons, R. (2010). Transaction-cost economics: Past, present, and future? *The Scandinavian Journal of Economics*, 112, 263–288.

Grubel, H. and Lloyd, P. (1975). *Intra-industry trade*. London: Macmillan.

Grüne-Yanoff, T. and Marchionni, C. (2018). Modeling model selection in model pluralism., *Journal of Economic Methodology*, 25(3), 265–275.

Hacking, I. (1983). *Representing and intervening: Introductory topics in the philosophy of natural science*. Cambridge: Cambridge University Press.

Hands, D. W. (2015). Orthodox and heterodox economics in recent economic methodology. *Erasmus Journal for Philosophy and Economics*, 8, 61–81.

Harris, R. (1984). Applied general equilibrium analysis of small open economies with scale economies and imperfect competition. *American Economic Review*, 74, 1016–1032.

Helpman, E. (1981). International trade in the presence of product differentiation, Economies of scale, and monopolistic competition: A Chamberlin–Heckscher–Ohlin model. *Journal of International Economics*, 11, 305–340.

Helpman, E. (1987). Imperfect competition and international trade: Evidence from fourteen industrial countries. *Journal of the Japanese and International Economies*, 1, 62–81.

Helpman, E. and Krugman, P. (1985). *Market structure and foreign trade: Increasing returns, imperfect competition and the international economy*, Cambridge, MA: MIT Press.

Khosrowi, D. (2019). Extrapolation of causal effects – hopes, assumptions, and the extrapolator's circle. *Journal of Economic Methodology*, 26, 45–58.

Khosrowi, D. (2021). What's (successful) extrapolation? *Journal of Economic Methodology*, 22, 140-152.

Kirman, A. (2016). Complexity and economic policy: A paradigm shift or a change in perspective? A review essay on David Colander and Roland Kupers' Complexity and the art of public policy. *Journal of Economic Literature*, 54, 534–572.

Kravis, I. (1971). The current case for import limitations. In: *Commission on International Trade and Investment Policy, United States Economic Policy in an Interdependent World*. Washington, DC: US Government Printing Office.

Krugman, P. (1979). Increasing returns, monopolistic competition, and international trade. *Journal of International Economics*, 9, 469–479.

Krugman, P. (1980). Scale economies, product differentiation, and the pattern of trade. *American Economic Review*, 70, 950–959.

Krugman, P. (1981). Intraindustry specialization and the gains from trade. *Journal of Political Economy*, 89, 959–973.

Kuhn, T. S. (1970 [1962]). *The structure of scientific revolutions*, Second edition, enlarged. Chicago: University of Chicago Press.

Lakatos, I. and Musgrave A. (eds) (1970). *Criticism and the growth of knowledge*. Cambridge: Cambridge University Press.

Lancaster, K. J. (1980). Intraindustry trade under perfect monopolistic competition. *Journal of International Economics*, 10, 151–175.

Laudan, L. (1977). *Progress and its problems: Towards a theory of scientific growth*. Berkeley: University of California Press.

Leamer, E. and Levinsohn, J. (1995). International trade theory: The evidence. In G. Grossman and K. Rogoff (eds), *Handbook of international economics*, Vol. 3. Amsterdam: Elsevier Science, 1341–1393.

Lehtinen, A. (2016). Introduction. In A. Lehtinen, J. Kuorikoski, and P. Ylikoski (eds), *Economics for real: Uskali Mäki and the place of truth in economics*. New York: Routledge.

Lehtinen, A., Kuorikoski, J., and Ylikoski, P. (eds) (2016). *Economics for real: Uskali Mäki and the place of truth in economics*. New York: Routledge.

Lind, H. (1992). A case study of normal research in theoretical economics. *Economics and Philosophy*, 8, 83-102.

Lind, H. (1993a). The myth of institutionalist method. *Journal of Economic Issues*, 27, 1–17.

Lind, H. (1993b). A note on fundamental theory and idealizations in Economics and Physics. *The British Journal for the Philosophy of Science*, 44(3), 493–503.

Lind, H. (2001). Rent regulation: A conceptual and comparative analysis. *European Journal of Housing Policy*, 1, 41–57.

Lind, H. (2003). Rent regulation and new construction: With a focus on Sweden 1995-2001. *Swedish Economic Policy Review*, 10, 135–167.

Lind, H. (2007). The story and the model done: An evaluation of mathematical models of rent control story and model. *Regional Science and Urban Economics*, 37, 183–198.

Lindbeck, A. (1985). The prize in economic science in memory of Alfred Nobel. *Journal of Economic Literature*, 23, 37–56.

Lindbeck, A. (2001). The Sveriges Riksbank prize in economic sciences in memory of Alfred Nobel 1969-2007. https:// www .nobelprize .org/ nobel _prizes/ themes/ economic-sciences/lindbeck/. Older version In A. Wallin-Levinovitz and N. Ringertz (eds) (2001). *The Nobel Prize; The First 100 Years*. Oxford: Imperial College Press.

Luyendijk, J. (2015). Don't let the Nobel prize fool you. Economics is not a science. *The Guardian*, 11 October 2015.

Karier, T. (2010). *Intellectual capital: Forty years of the Nobel Prize in Economics*. Cambridge: Cambridge University Press.

Mahoney, N. (2022). Principles for combining descriptive and model-based analysis in applied microeconomics research. *Journal of Economic Perspectives*, 36(3), 211–222.

Marchionni, C. (2013). Playing with networks: How economists explain. *European Journal of Philosophy of Science*, 3, 331–352.

McCloskey, D. (1983). The rhetoric of economics. *Journal of Economic Literature*, 21, 481–517.

McCloskey, D. (1994). *Knowledge and persuasion in economics*. Cambridge: Cambridge University Press.

McCloskey, D. N. (2021). *Bettering humanomics: A new, and old, approach to economic science*. Chicago: The University of Chicago Press.

McCloskey, D. N. (2022). *Beyond positivism, behaviorism, and neoinstitutionalism in economics*. Chicago: The University of Chicago Press.

Mäki, U. (2009). MISSing the world. Models as isolations and credible surrogate systems. *Erkenntnis*, 70, 29–43.

Neary, J. P. (2009). Putting the "new" into new trade theory: Paul Krugman's Nobel memorial prize in economics. *The Scandinavian Journal of Economics*, 111, 217–250.

Offer, A. and Söderberg, G. (2016). *The Nobel factor. The Prize in Economics, Social Democracy, and the market turn.* Princeton: Princeton University Press.

Ohlin, B. (1933). *Interregional and international trade.* Cambridge, MA: Harvard University Press.

Ostrom, E. (2000). Collective action and the evolution of social norms. *Journal of Economic Perspectives*, 14, 137–158.

Ostrom, E. Walker, J., and Gardner, R. (1992). Covenants with and without a sword: Self-Governance is possible. *The American Political Science Review*, 86, 404–417.

Purvis, D. (1982). James Tobin's contributions of economics. *The Scandinavian Journal of Economics*, 85, 61–88.

Rickles, D., Hawe, P., and Shiell, A. (2007). A simple guide to chaos and complexity. *Journal of Epidemial Community Health*, 61, 933–937.

Rodrik, D. (2015). *Economics rules: The rights and wrongs of the dismal science.* New York: W.W. Norton.

Rodrik, D. (2018). Second thoughts on economics rules. *Journal of Economic Methodology*, 25, 276–281.

Sandmo, A. (1993). Gary Becker's contribution to Economics. *The Scandinavian Journal of Economics*, 95, 7–23.

Schmalensee, R. (1983). George Stigler's contributions to economics. *The Scandinavian Journal of Economics*, 85, 77–86.

Solomon, M. (2011). Just a paradigm: Evidence-based medicine in epistemological context. *European Journal of Philosophy of Science*, 1, 451–466.

Sugden, R. (2000). Credible worlds: The status of theoretical models in economics. *Journal of Economic Methodology*, 7, 1–31.

Tadelis, S. (2013). *Game theory: An introduction.* Princeton, USA and Oxford, UK: Princeton University Press.

Todd, P. E. and Wolpin, K. I. (2023). The best of both worlds: Combining randomized controlled trials with structural modelling. *Journal of Economic Literature*, 61, 41–85.

University of Oxford, INET Oxford's Programme Complexity Economics. https://www.inet.ox.ac.uk/research/programmes/complexity-economics/

van Damme, Er and Weibull, J. W. (1995). Equilibrium in strategic interaction: The Contribution of John C. Harsanyi, John F. Nash and Reinhard Selten. *The Scandinavian Journal of Economics*, 97, 15–40.

Varian, H. R. (1984). Gerard Debreu's contribution to economics. *The Scandinavian Journal of Economics*, 86, 4–14.

Veit, W. (2021) Model diversity and the embarrassment of riches, *Journal of Economic Methodology*, 28, 291–303.

Williamson, O. E. (1971). The vertical integration of production: Market failure considerations. *American Economic Review, Papers and Proceedings*, 61, 112–123.

Williamson, O. E. (1976). Franchise bidding for natural monopolies – in general and with respect to CATV. *The Bell Journal of Economics*, 7, 73–104.

Index